MW01130062

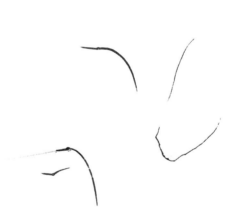

WORLD
HISTORY SERIES

The Punic Wars

Titles in the World History Series

WORLD
HISTORY SERIES ▪▪▪

The Punic Wars

by
Don Nardo

Lucent Books, P.O. Box 289011, San Diego, CA 92198-9011

Library of Congress Cataloging-in-Publication Data

Nardo, Don, 1947–
    The Punic Wars / by Don Nardo
        p. cm.—(World history series)
    Includes bibliographical references and index.
    ISBN 1-56006-417-X (Lib. ed.   :   alk. paper)
    1. Punic Wars—Juvenile literature.   I. Title.   II. Series.
DG242.N37   1996
937'.04—dc20   95-11713
                                                       CIP

Contents

Foreword

Each year on the first day of school, nearly every history teacher faces the task of explaining why his or her students should study history. One logical answer to this question is that exploring what happened in our past explains how the things we often take for granted—our customs, ideas, and institutions—came to be. As statesman and historian Winston Churchill put it, "Every nation or group of nations has its own tale to tell. Knowledge of the trials and struggles is necessary to all who would comprehend the problems, perils, challenges, and opportunities which confront us today." Thus, a study of history puts modern ideas and institutions in perspective. For example, though the founders of the United States were talented and creative thinkers, they clearly did not invent the concept of democracy. Instead, they adapted some democratic ideas that had originated in ancient Greece and with which the Romans, the British, and others had experimented. An exploration of these cultures, then, reveals their very real connection to us through institutions that continue to shape our daily lives.

Another reason often given for studying history is the idea that lessons exist in the past from which contemporary societies can benefit and learn. This idea, although controversial, has always been an intriguing one for historians. Those that agree that society can benefit from the past often quote philosopher George Santayana's famous statement, "Those who cannot remember the past are condemned to repeat it." Historians who ascribe to Santayana's philosophy believe that, for example, studying the events that led up to the major world wars or other significant historical events would allow society to chart a different and more favorable course in the future.

Just as difficult as convincing students to realize the importance of studying history is the search for useful and interesting supplementary materials that present historical events in a context that can be easily understood. The volumes in Lucent Books' World History Series attempt to present a broad, balanced, and penetrating view of the march of history. Ancient Egypt's important wars and rulers, for example, are presented against the rich and colorful backdrop of Egyptian religious, social, and cultural developments. The series engages the reader by enhancing historical events with these cultural contexts. For example, in *Ancient Greece*, the text covers the role of women in that society. Slavery is discussed in *The Roman Empire*, as well as how slaves earned their freedom. The numerous and varied aspects of everyday life in these and other societies are explored in each volume of the series. Additionally, the series covers the major political, cultural, and philosophical ideas as the torch of civilization is passed from ancient Mesopotamia and Egypt, through Greece, Rome, Medieval Europe, and other world cultures, to the modern day.

The material in the series is formatted in a thorough, precise, and organized manner. Each volume offers the reader a comprehensive and clearly written overview of an important historical event or period. The topic under discussion is placed in a broad historical context. For example, *The Italian Renaissance* begins with a discussion of the High Middle Ages and the loss of central control that allowed certain Italian cities to develop artistically. The book ends by looking forward to the Reformation and interpreting the societal changes that grew out of the Renaissance. Thus, students are not only involved in an historical era, but also enveloped by the events leading up to that era and the events following it.

One important and unique feature in the World History Series is the primary and secondary source quotations that richly supplement each volume. These quotes are useful in a number of ways. First, they allow students access to sources they would not normally be exposed to because of the difficulty and obscurity of the original source. The quotations range from interesting anecdotes to farsighted cultural perspectives and are drawn from historical witnesses both past and present. Second, the quotes demonstrate how and where historians themselves derive their information on the past as they strive to reach a consensus on historical events. Lastly, all of the quotes are footnoted, familiarizing students with the citation process and allowing them to verify quotes and/or look up the original source if the quote piques their interest.

Finally, the books in the World History Series provide a detailed launching point for further research. Each book contains a bibliography specifically geared toward student research. A second, annotated bibliography introduces students to all the sources the author consulted when compiling the book. A chronology of important dates gives students an overview, at a glance, of the topic covered. Where applicable, a glossary of terms is included.

In short, the series is designed not only to acquaint readers with the basics of history, but also to make them aware that their lives are a part of an ongoing human saga. Perhaps they will then come to the same realization as famed historian Arnold Toynbee. In his monumental work, *A Study of History*, he wrote about becoming aware of history flowing through him in a mighty current, and of his own life "welling like a wave in the flow of this vast tide."

Important Dates in the History of the Punic Wars

B.C.	2000	850	800	750	700	650	600	550

B.C.

ca. 2000–1000
Latin-speaking tribes, including the Romans, descend from central Europe into Italy; by 1000, Roman villages exist on the hills near the Tiber River in west-central Italy

ca. 850
Phoenician traders establish Carthage at the tip of Tunisia in northern Africa

ca. 800
The Etruscans settle Etruria in northwestern Italy

ca. 750
The Roman villages unite into a central town called Rome; the Greeks begin colonizing Sicily and southern Italy

ca. 640–610
The Etruscans take control of Rome

509
The Romans expel their Etruscan king and establish the Roman Republic

ca. 300–275
Carthage is recognized as undisputed naval master of the western Mediterranean

ca. 290
The Romans complete their conquest of central Italy

280
Pyrrhus, king of the Greek state of Epirus, comes to the aid of the Italian Greek cities, who fear subjugation by Rome

275
Pyrrhus withdraws his forces from Italy, leaving the Greeks to fight their own battles

265
Rome completes conquest of the Italian Greek cities, becoming master of all Italy south of the Po Valley

264
Carthage takes control of the strategic Strait of Messina between Italy and Sicily; in response, Rome declares war on Carthage, initiating the First Punic War

260
The Romans win a decisive naval victory against Carthage near Mylae in northern Sicily

256
In the largest sea battle of ancient times, fought near Cape Ecnomus in southern Sicily, the Romans cripple the Carthaginian fleet, leaving the northern African coast defenseless

255
Carthage hires the Greek mercenary commander Xanthippus, who defeats the invasion forces of Roman consul Marcus Regulus in the Bagradas Valley, south of Carthage; Rome loses over two hundred ships to a huge storm off the coast of Sicily

249–242
Carthage's war leader Hamilcar Barca successfully harasses Roman positions on the Italian and Sicilian coasts

241
After throwing all its remaining resources into building one last fleet, Rome defeats Carthage off the western Sicilian coast; Carthage sues for peace, ending the First Punic War

241–239
Hamilcar fights and defeats an army of former Carthaginian mercenaries in the "Truceless War"

238
Rome initiates a policy of imperialism by annexing the Carthaginian-controlled islands of Sardinia and Corsica

237
Hamilcar begins the conquest of southern Spain in an effort to carve out a Carthaginian kingdom there

229
Hamilcar dies in a drowning accident; his son-in-law Hasdrubal inherits his power in Spain

226
Hasdrubal reluctantly signs a treaty with Rome, promising not to cross the Jucar River in east-central Spain

225–220
Rome defeats the Gauls in the Po Valley, extending Roman influence over all Italian lands south of the Alps

221
Hasdrubal is murdered and Hannibal, Hamilcar's son, succeeds him

220–219
Hannibal besieges and captures Saguntum, a Roman ally on the east coast of Spain

218
Carthage refuses to surrender Hannibal and the Romans declare war, initiating the Second Punic War; Hannibal crosses the Alps into Italy and defeats the Romans at the Trebia River

217
Hannibal defeats the Romans at Lake Trasimene, seventy miles north of Rome; the Romans appoint Fabius Maximus dictator to deal with the emergency

216
Hannibal is triumphant again as, in the worst single military defeat in its history, Rome loses over fifty thousand men in a great battle near Cannae, in southeastern Italy

215
Hannibal makes an alliance with King Philip V of Macedonia, who promises to invade Italy

214
The Romans defeat Philip at Apollonia, in Illyria; the city of Syracuse allies itself with Hannibal

212
After a long siege, highlighted by a plague that strikes both sides and the use against the Romans of ingenious mechanical weapons invented by Syracusan scientist Archimedes, Syracuse falls to Rome

211
The Romans recapture Capua, on the western Italian coast, which had defected to Hannibal, and also Saguntum in Spain.

208–207
Hannibal's brother, Hasdrubal Barca, leads an army from Spain over the Alps and into northern Italy; soon afterward, the Romans decisively defeat Hasdrubal near the Metaurus River

206
The young Scipio defeats the Carthaginians at Ilipa, in southern Spain, ending Carthage's reign over the region

204
Scipio invades northern Africa and lays siege to Utica, about twenty-five miles from Carthage

203
Hannibal abandons Italy and lands his army in northern Africa

202
Scipio defeats Hannibal on the plain of Zama, ending the war; Carthage is forced to give up most of its Mediterranean possessions, burn most of its warships, and pay Rome a huge yearly war indemnity

200–197
The Second Macedonian War; Rome conquers Macedonia, fulfilling its revenge against King Philip for helping Hannibal

195
Rome accuses Hannibal of conspiring with its enemies and he flees to the eastern Mediterranean

183
Hannibal dies by suicide in exile; Scipio dies in Italy

154
The Numidians, under Masinissa, come to blows with the Carthaginians over disputed North African territory

150
Carthage's general Hasdrubal fights a great battle with Masinissa

149
Claiming that by making war on Masinissa, Carthage is violating the treaty ending the previous war, Rome initiates the Third Punic War and invades Africa; Carthage offers stiff resistance, delivering the Roman invaders several defeats

147
Scipio Aemilianus, adopted grandson of the Scipio who defeated Hannibal, takes command of Rome's forces and begins a siege of Carthage

146
The Romans overrun Carthage and raze the city, forever eradicating the Carthaginian culture

The Frightening Specter of World War

The concept of world war is both awesome and frightening. All the world's major powers took part in the great conflicts known as World War I (1914–1918) and World War II (1939–1945); many nations suffered widespread devastation, and tens of millions of people lost their lives. These wars were distinguished by their use of modern weapons of mass destruction and by their sheer vastness. In many people's minds, such factors seemed to set them apart from all the conflicts that occurred before the twentieth century.

And yet, in a sense, these modern wars were not the first world wars to rock civilization. That distinction belongs to the Punic Wars, fought in the third and second centuries B.C. between Rome and Carthage, the two great military powers of that time. The Roman-Carthaginian struggles utilized the most advanced weapons of that era, including a brand new and very effective "secret" weapon. And these conflicts were long lasting and huge in scale. According to the second-century B.C. Greek/Roman historian Polybius, the First Punic War "lasted without a break for twenty-four years and is the longest . . . and greatest war we know of."[1] Indeed, Rome's casualties at sea in this conflict alone constituted the greatest naval losses by any single nation in world history—far

larger, in fact, than the naval losses of all the World War II combatants combined.

Rome and Carthage

To be sure, the Punic Wars, unlike their modern counterparts, were not truly global. In that ancient era, civilized societies existed in China, central Africa, Japan, and Central America, and none took part in, or in all likelihood even knew about, the Roman-Carthaginian struggles. Yet these societies were largely isolated from and had no influence on the world's main civilized region—the lands surrounding the Mediterranean Sea. Here could be found humanity's oldest, most populous, and most powerful interacting cultures, among them those of Greece, Egypt, Rome, and Carthage. At the time, the Mediterranean world was, for all intents and purposes, the "known world." The epic Second Punic War, a death struggle between that world's two greatest powers, either involved or affected the immediate futures of all the lands stretching from Spain to the Middle East. Thus in a very real sense the conflict was indeed a world war. Certainly, for the residents of Rome or Carthage it presented just as much danger of destroying civilization as they knew it as World War II did for people of our time.

But while the ancient and modern world wars were largely equivalent in their overall scope, drama, and devastation, the intent of the combatants differed in the two historical periods. The major difference between the older and newer wars was in the attitudes and ultimate goals of those who fought them. As classical historian Dorothy Mills explains:

> There was one great difference between ancient and modern times. One of the greatest problems that the world today is trying to solve is how great and powerful nations can live side by side in peace and friendship. The ancient world had not discovered that such a state of affairs was even possible. To the statesmen and thinkers of those days it seemed natural and right that one great and powerful state should have dominion over those that were weaker, and so when Rome and Carthage found that their interests were in conflict with one another, there was only one question between them to be settled: one must rule, the other obey, and such a question could only be settled by war.[2]

That victory in such a war might be the first step in a policy of world domination was almost taken for granted at the time. Indeed, plenty of precedent existed for such aggressive policy. The Persians, a Middle Eastern people, had attempted to overrun the known world in the sixth and fifth centuries B.C. And a century later Greek conqueror Alexander the Great

The two greatest generals of the Punic Wars—Carthage's Hannibal Barca and Rome's Scipio Africanus—in their historic meeting before the decisive battle of Zama in 202 B.C.

had tried to do the same. The winner in the Roman-Carthaginian struggle for Mediterranean dominance would be the next logical contender for world supremacy. In a contest with such high stakes, to display any sign of weakness would have been a fatal mistake. The weaker combatant ran the risk not only of losing the war, but also of suffering total annihilation. Thus it was in the years before the third and final Punic War. Carthage, already twice defeated by Rome, made the mistake of trying merely to live in peace with its former enemy and for this error paid a heavy price. According to military scholar Arleigh Burke:

> Rome set out to reduce the power and influence of Carthage and eventually to destroy her. Rome succeeded, step by little step, because Carthage . . . was convinced that since [another] war would be expensive to all participants, the Romans would not resort to war. . . . Only it did not work out this way. . . . Too late—much too late—the Carthaginians realized the significance of their past actions and the end that threatened them and their civilization.[3]

Carthage, the first major loser of a world war, was totally destroyed and disappeared from the pages of history. Here again, the major difference between ancient and modern world wars is apparent. After defeating Germany and Japan in World War II, the United States and its allies sought to rebuild their former enemies and help them to become productive partners. The Romans did the opposite: with brutal efficiency, they ensured that they would never have to deal with the Carthaginians again. And in so doing,

The Romans slaughter the inhabitants of Carthage, one of the great cities of the ancient world, in the devastating conclusion of the Third Punic War.

Rome cleared the way for its spectacular rise to dominion over the entire Mediterranean world. In short, Rome succeeded by eliminating its rival, while the victors in World War II succeeded by making friends with theirs. Whether the modern version constitutes an advancement in human affairs is debatable. The real question is whether the frightening specter of world war, first unleashed before the battlements of Rome and Carthage, will ever be eliminated. And the answer to this fateful question depends on the wisdom or folly of future generations.

Chapter

1 Ancient Rivalry: The Western Mediterranean on the Eve of War

In the early third century B.C., the nations of Rome and Carthage were the two leading economic and military powers in the western Mediterranean region. The cities themselves were separated by only 350 miles of open sea, and each was located in a strategic geographic position. Rome occupied a cluster of low hills at a bend in the Tiber River, about 15 miles inland from the western coast of Italy. Carthage was situated almost directly south, on a peninsula at the northern tip of what is now Tunisia in northern Africa. Tunisia, the Italian "boot," and Sicily, the large island lying at the foot of the boot, effectively divide the Mediterranean into two spheres. An expanse of sea less than a hundred miles wide between Tunisia and Sicily, and the narrow Strait of Messina between Italy and Sicily, are the only water channels connecting the eastern and western spheres. Therefore, both Rome and Carthage held commanding positions. With sufficient naval power, either one could easily police the two channels and exploit and control the western Mediterranean.

Overpowering desire for such exploitation and control led to rivalry and, eventually, armed conflict between Rome and Carthage. Between 264 and 146 B.C., these nations engaged in a series of epic struggles known as the Punic Wars. The term "Punic" comes from the Latin word *Punicus*, meaning Phoenician, the name of the Middle Eastern people who originally settled Carthage in approximately 850 B.C. These three long and costly wars constituted a bitter, all-out struggle for survival between the Roman and Carthaginian peoples. The outcome of this struggle sealed the fate of one and ensured for many years the uncontested control of the western Mediterranean for the other. Because this outcome had a major influence on the future of Mediterranean and European civilization, the Punic Wars, seen as a whole, constitute one of the most decisive events in history.

Competing Spheres of Influence

The desire for control of the western Mediterranean did not begin in the third century B.C. and was not confined to Rome and Carthage. In fact, in the preceding five centuries the region had witnessed a bitter ancient rivalry among four competing spheres of influence—Roman, Carthaginian, Etruscan, and Greek. The Etruscans were a culturally advanced and somewhat mysterious people who, about 800 B.C., settled in the fertile plains and hills north of Rome, an area that became known as Etruria. Skilled in pottery and other crafts, the Etruscans traded their wares with less advanced peoples throughout much of northern Italy. They also carried on a thriving trade with the inhabitants of Sardinia and Corsica, the large islands located directly west of Italy, as well as with other Mediterranean regions.

Not long after the Etruscans arrived in northern Italy, large Greek cities such as Athens and Miletus began colonizing southern Italy and Sicily. The Greek cities of Naxos and Syracuse, both in Sicily, were established in 757 and 735, respectively. Cumae, in southwestern Italy, was settled in 725, and Tarentum, at the bottom of the Italian boot, in 708. After a century of colonization, there were so many Greek towns in southern Italy that the Romans began calling the area *Magna Graecia*, or "Greater Greece." Like the Etruscans, the Greeks competed vigorously for shares in the lucrative trade routes running north-south through Italy and east-west through the Mediterranean. And for more than two centuries, the two peoples largely controlled these routes. But over time that control increasingly fell into the hands of the Romans and Carthaginians, both of whom had been living in the region when the Etruscans and Greeks arrived.

Roman Villages Unite

The Romans were among a group of Latin-speaking tribes that had descended in waves from central Europe into Italy beginning about 2000 B.C. By 1000, the

The painting on these shards of an Etruscan vase, as in most Etruscan pottery, shows a strong Greek influence.

Romans had built villages on the hills at the bend in the Tiber River on the northern edge of the fertile plain of Latium. This plain was bordered in the west by the sea and in the east by the rugged Appenine Mountains, which run north to south through the Italian boot. In about 750, these villages united into a single large town called Rome. The Romans, at the time largely uncultured rustic farmers, came increasingly under the influence of their more advanced neighbors, the Etruscans. "It is clear," writes classical scholar Gavin de Beer,

> that the Etruscans made an important contribution to the customs, institutions, and language of the Romans. . . . Many of the inventions and innovations commonly attributed to the Romans were adopted by them directly from the Etruscans, who devised the vaulted arch, drains, and the rectangular lay-out of town planning. So-called

Roman numerals are Etruscan numerals; Etruscans introduced the facses [ax-head tied to a bundle of sticks] and the double-headed ax as symbols of constituted authority, eagles as standards for the army . . . the purple toga for chief magistrates [government officials] . . . gladiatorial fights, and public triumphs [victory parades].[4]

The Etruscans apparently also introduced political ideas to the Romans. The Romans copied the Etruscan concept of rule by kings, and the first Roman king, possibly named Romulus, came to power at about the same time that the Roman villages united into a central town. In the seventh century B.C., however, the Etruscans exercised their superior power and installed their own kings in Rome. Under direct Etruscan rule, the rude Romans became a bit more cultured and replaced many of their primitive wooden huts and dirt roads with stone buildings and paved streets. According to historian H. H. Scullard:

One outstanding aspect of the growth of the city under the Etruscans is its amazing speed: within a century a collection of huts had developed into a city with a civic center [the Forum], public buildings and temples of which the greatest could vie with any in Etruria and indeed in the contemporary Greek world.[5]

The Arrogant, Reasonable Romans

The Etruscans may have been more cultured than the Romans. But they were not nearly as adaptable, resourceful, or innately aggressive. Sick of Etruscan rule, in 509 B.C. the Romans boldly threw out the Etruscan king and established the Roman Republic, in which the government was

A meeting of the early Roman Senate. Before the republic, the Senate was composed of elders known as senatores, who held no real power and acted merely as advisors to the kings. By contrast, in republican times the Senate largely controlled Rome's government.

run by representatives elected by the people. The Romans defined "the people" rather narrowly, however: Only free adult males, a small proportion of the population, could vote and hold public office. A group of these citizens met periodically in a body known as the Assembly to propose and vote on laws; once a year they elected two consuls, or chief administrators, to run the state. Another legislative body, the Senate, was made up exclusively of well-to-do landowners. The senators directly advised the consuls and, taking advantage of their wealth and position, indirectly influenced the Assembly. In effect, therefore, the Senate was the real power in Rome and the republic was an oligarchy—a government run by an elite few—rather than a democracy.

Nevertheless, the Roman Republic proved to be both flexible and popular and largely met the needs of the people. Most Romans came to view their system with pride and patriotism. Practical, hard working, and used to coping with difficulties, they came to see themselves as destined to rule others. Part of this arrogant attitude came from their religion. The Romans worshiped a pantheon, or group of gods, some of which were nature spirits prayed to by Roman farmers since the days of the first settlement in Latium. Many other Roman gods were adopted from the Etruscan and Greek pantheons. The chief Roman god was Jupiter, whose wife, Juno, was goddess of women and childbirth. Neptune was ruler of the sea, Mars the guardian of fields and crops and also overseer of war, and Apollo the god of the sun, music, healing, and prophecy. Inherent in Roman religion was the idea that these and Rome's other gods favored the Romans above all other peoples. Therefore, it seemed only

Roman defenders hold off an Etruscan attack force during one of the early struggles between the two peoples. Rome eventually prevailed and absorbed the Etruscans into its growing empire.

natural for Rome to seek political, economic, and cultural supremacy.

Beginning in the fifth century B.C., Roman armies marched outward from Latium and began subduing neighboring peoples, including their former rulers, the Etruscans. Among the many powerful hill tribes conquered by Rome were the Aequi, the Volsci, the Sabines, and the warlike and well-organized Samnites, who inhabited the Apennines in south-central Italy. The Romans had a genius for political organization, and early on the key to their growing power was their lenient treatment of conquered peoples. They

"Romanized" such peoples, introducing the Latin language and Roman customs; but more importantly, they formed long-lasting alliances with the vanquished tribes and farmers. "What made the Romans so remarkable," says classical historian Michael Grant, was

> a talent for patient political reasonableness that was unique in the ancient world. . . . On the whole, Rome found it advisable . . . to keep its bargains with its allies, displaying a self-restraint, a readiness to compromise, and a calculated generosity that the world had never seen. And so the allies, too, had little temptation to feel misused. The proud Samnites, it is true, had lost a considerable amount of their land to Roman settlers. . . . But they were only a few out of a grand total of one hundred and twenty Italian communities with which Rome, in due course, formed perpetual alliances. After the end of the Samnite wars [about 290 B.C.] a network of such agreements was extended across the whole of central Italy.[6]

Master of Italy

In the 280s B.C., Rome's dominion over south-central Italy brought it into close contact with the Greek-controlled lands making up the southern third of the Italian boot. Having conquered the Etruscans, their chief northern rival, the Romans now sought to do the same to their chief southern rival. The most powerful of the mainland Greek cities was Tarentum, located on the southern Italian coast. At the time, Tarentum was larger than Rome and possessed the biggest fleet in all of Italy. Rome, still largely a land power, had very few ships, but in 282 boldly sent most of them to establish a military base not far from Tarentum. The worried Tarentines responded by destroying the ships and killing the Roman commander.

The inhabitants of Tarentum and neighboring independent Greek city-states knew full well that the Romans would retaliate by sending large, formidable armies south. The Greeks also realized that their own land armies were small, ill trained, and lacking in overall unity and effective organization. So they appealed for help to another Greek state, Epirus, in extreme northwestern Greece. The Epirote king, Pyrrhus, a renowned general with a large, well-trained army, accepted the invitation

Pyrrhus (319–272 B.C.) became king of the Greek kingdom of Epirus at the age of twelve. Like other Greek military commanders, he utilized the famed and deadly Macedonian phalanx formation.

to defend the Italian Greeks against Rome. According to Michael Grant:

> The basis of Pyrrhus's force was a phalanx [battle formation] of twenty thousand men. In battle, lined up in depth, they displayed a front that bristled with the heads of their long lances, as impenetrable as a barbed wire entanglement; and their task was to hold the Roman army while their cavalry [troops on horseback] on the wings turned [swung around behind] its rear or flank. Pyrrhus also brought with him a contingent of twenty frightening Indian war-elephants, which he used not frontally like tanks as was the custom, but laterally [on the sides], so that they could join the horsemen in attacking the enemy's flanks.[7]

In 280 Pyrrhus marched his forces into Italy. Thanks partly to the terror and disruption his elephants spread through the ranks of the enemy's cavalry, he defeated the Romans at Heraclea, a Greek town near Tarentum. But the Romans were skilled and stubborn fighters and even in defeat inflicted heavy casualties on Pyrrhus's army. Pyrrhus continued to enjoy victories against Roman forces, but like the first, each one proved unusually costly

Pyrrhus's men and elephants are caught up in the bloody turmoil of battle in one of their impressive but costly "pyrrhic" victories over the skilled Roman forces.

for the Epirotes. At last, in 275, Pyrrhus decided to cut his losses and return to Greece, in effect abandoning the Italian Greeks. One by one, over the next decade, the Greek cities in Italy submitted to Roman domination. By 265, Rome was undisputed master of all of Italy, except for the Po Valley in the far north, near the towering peaks of the Alps.

The Bold Phoenicians

In less than three centuries, Rome had risen from a small city-state controlling only a few hundred square miles of territory to one of the largest and strongest Mediterranean powers. During these years of expansion, the Romans had managed to absorb the Etruscans and the Italian Greeks. This eliminated two of the three major cultural spheres with which Rome competed for influence in the western Mediterranean. Stronger and more confident than ever, the Romans now began considering expansion beyond the Italian mainland, and in the process put themselves face-to-face with the region's remaining great power—Carthage. Rome would soon find Carthage the most formidable foe it had ever encountered.

Like Rome, Carthage began as a small, unimposing town that gave no hint of the power and glory it would attain. Sometime in the mid-ninth century B.C., Phoenician merchants landed on the shores at the northern tip of Tunisia and established Carthage as a modest trading post. The homeland of the Phoenicians, who were related to the Hebrews and other Middle Eastern peoples, was along the coasts of what is now Lebanon at the eastern edge

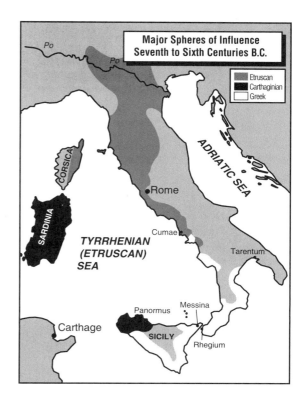

of the Mediterranean. "Like Greece, Italy, and Sicily," writes historian Donald Armstrong, "Phoenicia comprised many independent city-states, each ruled by its own king and each rarely larger than a small American county. Tyre, though it was the most important of the Phoenician kingdoms, had a perimeter of a mere two and a half miles."[8]

The Phoenicians were primarily sailors, who, between the ninth and seventh centuries B.C., were the boldest explorers and wealthiest merchants in the Mediterranean. In addition to Carthage, they founded colonies and trading posts that ringed the western end of the sea. These included Utica and Hadrumetum [later Sousse], both near Carthage in northern Africa; Panormus [later Palermo] and Motya in western Sicily;

Phoenician merchants trade at an outdoor marketplace. The Phoenicians excelled in gold working, ivory carving, and metal engraving, and their wares were in demand throughout the Mediterranean.

Nora and Tharros in Sardinia; Abdera and Malaca [modern-day Málaga] in southern Spain; and Gades [later Cadiz], also in southern Spain but beyond the Strait of Gibraltar on the Atlantic coast. As scholars Gilbert and Colette Picard explain:

> All the available information about the Phoenician method of colonization shows that it differed radically from that of the Greeks. By the Greek method, numerous groups of emigrants left their overcrowded motherland far behind them and settled in a new country with no thought of return. Then they set to work at once to re-create the image of their native Greece. The Phoenicians on the other hand sought merely to establish trading posts providing a safe port of call

for their ships, food and rest for their crews . . . and warehouses for such merchandise as was needed for bargaining with the natives.[9]

The Quest for Wealth

But Carthage did not remain a mere trading post for long. Over the years it grew in size and population, absorbed many of the other Phoenician colonies in the western Mediterranean, and founded new ones of its own. In this way, it continually expanded its trading network and became very wealthy. In fact, the quest for wealth was the basis of nearly all Carthaginian political and social policies. Unlike Rome, which expanded with the aim of controlling and influencing others, Carthage expanded almost solely to keep its upper classes rich and comfortable.

This money-based foreign policy was reflected in Carthage's government, as well. Like the Romans, the Carthaginians early got rid of their kings and installed a republic, although common Carthaginians had even less say in politics than their Roman counterparts. Carthage had a Council of Four Hundred, which was similar to the Roman Senate. In the Carthaginian version, however, the members were mainly wealthy merchants and traders rather than wealthy landowners. Carthage's Council was the supreme authority for the city and empire. It made the laws, punished wrongdoers, and decided local and foreign policy, all in a strict and often harsh manner, to ensure that the state's inflow of wealth remained uninterrupted. To carry out its commands, the Council periodically chose two administrators, called *suffetes*. The *suffetes* were somewhat equivalent to the

---

Beyond the Pillars of Hercules

The fifth century B.C. Greek historian Herodotus was well aware of the exploits of generations of Phoenician explorers. In addition to founding Carthage and other colonies on Mediterranean coasts, he explained in his Histories, *the Phoenicians sailed into the Indian and Atlantic Oceans and may even have circumnavigated the African continent.*

"I cannot but be surprised at the method of mapping Libya [Africa], Asia, and Europe. . . . As for Libya, we know that it is washed on all sides by the sea except where it joins Asia, as was first demonstrated . . . by the Egyptian king [pharaoh] Neco, who . . . sent out a fleet manned by a Phoenician crew with orders to sail around and return to Egypt and the Mediterranean by way of the Pillars of Hercules [Strait of Gibraltar]. The Phoenicians sailed from the Red Sea into the southern [Indian] ocean, and every autumn put in [went ashore] where they were on the Libyan coast, sowed a patch of ground, and waited for next year's harvest. Then, having got in [loaded] their grain, they put to sea again, and after two full years rounded the Pillars of Hercules in the course of the third, and returned to Egypt. These men made a statement which I do not myself believe, though others may, to the effect that as they sailed on a westerly course round the southern end of Libya, they had the sun on their right—to northward of them [an accurate description of the sun's position as seen from south of the equator; the Phoenicians' statement was correct]. This is how Libya was first discovered to be surrounded by sea, and the next people to make a similar report were the Carthaginians."

Before the outbreak of the Punic Wars, Carthaginian merchants barter for goods, including a female slave, with the wealthy owners of a Roman villa.

Roman consuls but lacked much of the power and prestige of the latter officials. The Council largely kept the *suffetes* and Carthaginian generals under its thumb. For example, it was not unusual for these leaders to face immediate crucifixion or some other gruesome form of execution merely for losing a battle or making a political or tactical error.

Religion played almost as large a role in the formulation of Carthage's state policy as did the acquisition of wealth. This was because, like their Phoenician forebears, the Carthaginians believed that all human misfortunes were the result of the wrath of the gods. If a battle was lost, it meant that a god was angry and whatever policy had led to the defeat should be abandoned. The gods also could be appeased by sacrifice. But in Carthage the form of sacrifice often differed radically from that in Etruscan, Greek, and Roman societies. In these European cultures the gods were seen as having primarily human form and characteristics, and sacrifices consisting of plants or animals usually sufficed to appease them. By contrast, the Carthaginian gods, among them Melkart, Tanit, and Baal, often were represented as demonic and monstrous. They were bloodthirsty and demanded human sacrifice. Thus, to atone for mistakes or misfortunes, the Carthaginians sacrificed children, sometimes hundreds at a time, by casting them into huge ceremonial fires.

Carthage's political and religious ideas and methods seemed unusually harsh and cruel to the Greeks, Romans, and other Mediterranean peoples. But the Carthaginians, even most commoners, accepted these ideas and methods as natural and necessary for maintaining the empire's prosperity. Therefore, Carthage had a stable government and an overriding religious framework that met most of the needs of the state and the people. And this arrangement enabled the empire continually to expand and thrive.

To be sure, the Carthaginians did encounter some obstacles along the way. For centuries, while Rome remained a land power preoccupied with conquering territory in Italy, Carthage's major economic and colonial rivals in the region were the Greeks. In addition to southern Italy and Sicily, the Greeks planted colonies on the southern coast of Gaul, what is now France, as well as on the eastern coast of Spain and on many nearby islands. The Carthaginians and Greeks often came to blows over competing colonies and financial interests. About 535 B.C., for instance, Carthage, aided by an Etruscan naval force, defeated a Greek fleet off the coast of Corsica. Because the Greek cities in the area, like Greek cities everywhere else, were notorious for their inability to unite, the

The Carthaginian fertility god, Baal, often called the "lord of the universe," holds a human baby. The sacrifice of children was a common ritual in this god's temples.

Carthaginians were able to outmaneuver and overshadow them. By the beginning of the third century, Carthage had become the undisputed commercial and naval master of the western Mediterranean.

Sizing Each Other Up

With Carthage in control of northern Africa and most of the islands and Rome master of Italy, the two nations had become the western Mediterranean's superpowers. The goal of each was to dominate the region, obviously at the other's expense. Consequently, there seemed little doubt in anyone's mind that these powers were destined to clash. The wily Pyrrhus summed it up well. According to the ancient Greek/Roman writer Plutarch, as Pyrrhus abandoned Italy and returned to Epirus in 275 B.C., he remarked, "How brave a field of war do we leave, my friends, for the Romans and Carthaginians to fight in."[10]

In anticipation of the coming struggle, some Roman and Carthaginian leaders undoubtedly began sizing each other up, and certain strengths and weaknesses were immediately apparent. First, Rome was mainly an agrarian, or farming, society and Carthage a seafaring one. The second most obvious difference lay in the size and splendor, or lack thereof, of the mother cities. In the early third century B.C. Rome was still a moderate-sized city, shabby and dirty, with few large stone buildings and a population of 50,000, perhaps as high as 75,000. In comparison, Carthage had a population of 100,000 to 200,000. And it was at least three times as large as Rome, more impressively laid out, and better maintained. As historian James Henry Breasted comments:

> The city of Carthage itself was large and splendid. . . . Behind wide docks and extensive piers of masonry, teeming with ships and merchandise, the city spread far inland, with spacious markets and busy manufacturing quarters humming with industry. Beyond the dwellings of the poorer craftsmen . . . rose the stately houses of the wealthy merchants, with luxuriant tropical gardens. Around the whole rose imposing walls and massive fortifications.[11]

In his *Roman History*, the Roman historian Appian provided this more contemporary and detailed description of Carthage's all-important harbors:

> The harbors were so arranged that ships could pass from one to the other. The entrance from the sea was 70 feet wide and could be closed by iron chains. The first harbor, reserved for merchant ships, had a large selection of berths [ship moorings]. In the center of the inner harbor was an island which . . . was lined with quays [docks] . . . providing accommodation

---

The Home of Many Goats

Many scholars believe that this description by the legendary Greek poet Homer, in his epic Odyssey, *depicts the future harbor, "admiral's island," and countryside of Carthage. Early Greek and/or Phoenician explorers of the tenth or ninth centuries B.C. evidently visited the then-virgin site and brought back accounts of what seemed to the Greeks of that time a faraway and exotic land.*

"Not very far from the harbor on [the]coast, and not so near either, there lies a luxuriant island, covered with woods, which is the home of innumerable goats. The goats are wild, for man has made no pathways that might frighten them off, nor do hunters visit the island with their hounds to rough it in the forests and to range the mountain-tops. . . . It is by no means a poor country, but capable of yielding any crop in due season. Along the shore of the grey sea there are soft water-meadows [marshes] where the vine would never wither; and there is plenty of land level enough for the plough, where [farmers] could count on cutting a deep crop at every harvest-time, for the soil below the surface is exceedingly rich. Also it has a safe harbor, in which there is no occasion to tie up [use ropes to secure the boat] at all. You need neither cast anchor nor make fast with hawsers [mooring cables]: all your crew have to do is to beach their boat and wait till the spirit moves them and the right wind blows. Finally, at the head of the harbor there is a stream of fresh water, running out of a cave in a grove of poplar-trees."

---

for 220 ships; above these were lofts for storing the rigging. In the front of each boat-house stood two Ionic columns, so that the perimeter of the harbor looked like a portico [elegant column-lined porch]. On the island itself stood a small building used as a headquarters for the admiral.[12]

Carthage appears to have been more populous than Rome as a nation as well as a city. The city-state of Carthage alone, comprising about eight thousand square miles of plains, hills, and farmland in northern Tunisia, held at least 700,000 people. Adding to this population the inhabitants of the empire's many colonies and allies may have brought Carthage's total human resources to 1.5 million. By contrast, the Romans and their Italian subject peoples numbered no more than a million, and less than a quarter were adult male citizens.

Power Was All That Mattered

However, Carthage's overall numerical advantage was deceiving. There can be no doubt that with its large fleets and long seafaring tradition, Carthage possessed the naval upper hand. Indeed, Rome had no navy at all. But having fewer people to draw on did not necessarily give Rome a disadvantage on land, too. For one thing, despite its large population, Carthage did not call on its citizens to fight. Carthaginian officers commanded the armies. But the troops themselves were mercenaries, or hired foreign soldiers, who, because they were not defending their own homes and families, did not always put their

hearts into their work. As the Picards explain:

> The Carthaginian armies had not such a good reputation as the navy. It was generally recognized that the citizens of Carthage . . . preferred to entrust the defense of their interests to professional soldiers. This custom, dating from before the sixth century, can be explained by their anxiety to preserve the city's manpower, which could not be easily replaced, and also by their conception of war as an extension of business. It would seem quite normal for them to entrust it to an agent.[13]

The Romans had at their disposal armies that were more dependable and much better trained and organized. These armies were made up of legions—groups of about forty-five hundred men—most of whom were citizen soldiers defending their state, their homes, and their families. This made them more loyal than paid foreign mercenaries, and more willing to stick out a tough campaign. And the structure and regimentation of the legions were superior to those of most other armies. According to Gavin de Beer, each legion was divided into ten smaller units called cohorts, and

> in each cohort there was one maniple [troop formation] of *hastati*, younger men, 120 in number, armed with sword, javelin, and lance; one maniple of *principes*, slightly older men, also 120 in number, similarly armed; and one maniple of *triarii*, mature middle-aged men, 60 in number, who were armed with sword and pike [spear] and constituted an old guard of veterans. . . . The mainstay of the Roman

To Terrify the Enemy

In his Histories, *the second century B.C. Greek/Roman historian Polybius goes into considerable detail about the troops, weapons, and organization of the Roman armies of his time. In this excerpt, he describes a soldier's panoply, or complete battle dress.*

"The Roman panoply consists firstly of a shield (*scutum*), the convex [outwardly curved] surface of which measures two and a half feet in width and four feet in length, the thickness at the rim being a palm's breadth. It is made of two planks glued together, the outer surface being then covered first with canvas and then with calf-skin. Its upper and lower rims are strengthened by an iron edging which protects it from descending blows and from injury when rested on the ground. It also has an iron boss (*umbo*) [outer coating] fixed to it which turns aside the more formidable blows of stones, pikes and heavy missiles in general. Besides the shield they also carry a sword, hanging on the right thigh and called a Spanish sword. This is excellent for thrusting, and both of its edges cut effectually, as the blade is very strong and firm. In addition they have

two *pila* [pikes], a brass helmet, and greaves [leg protectors]. The *pila* are of two sorts—stout and fine. . . . Each is fitted with a barbed iron head. . . . Finally they wear as an ornament a circle of feathers with three upright purple or black feathers about a cubit [twenty inches] in height . . . to make every man look twice his real height, and to give him a fine appearance, such as will strike terror into the enemy. The common soldiers wear in addition a breastplate of brass . . . which they place in front of the heart and call the heart-protector (*pectorale*), this completing their accoutrements [outfit].

The Roman soldier at far left holds a cornu, *a curved battle trumpet. His companion wears a* lorica segmentata, *a leather tunic with metal strips attached.*

In this depiction of a meeting in a Roman military camp, a commander briefs his general on the results of a mission while several signifers, *bearing the legion's insignia, and other troops look on.*

army was its wonderful centurions . . . tough, professional long-service senior . . . officers, two to a maniple, devoted to the army and to the state, who by their drill and discipline licked the legionnaries into shape.[14]

Thus, with Carthage having the advantage at sea and Rome the advantage on land, it is probably accurate to describe the two as being about equal in military strength on the eve of the First Punic War.

Perhaps if the opposing leaders could have foreseen the dreadful losses both sides would suffer in this titanic struggle, they would have avoided hostilities. But at the time, all that mattered to both nations was ultimate power over the western Mediterranean. And war seemed the natural and inevitable means to that end. All that was needed was an excuse to begin the fighting and, as it happened, that excuse was provided by a long-standing rival of both Rome and Carthage—the Greeks.

2 Once More into the Breach: The Death Struggle Begins

The First Punic War, which erupted in 264 B.C., was the largest and most devastating conflict fought anywhere on earth up to that time. It lasted for twenty-three years, caused hundreds of thousands of deaths, and exhausted both contenders—Rome and Carthage. One reason the war was so long and destructive was that both sides fought hard and stubbornly. Despite terrible losses and bitter disappointments, each one repeatedly bounced back and threw itself once more into the breach of battle. There can be little doubt that each party had severely underestimated the other's resources and abilities and overestimated its own. But the stakes they fought for were huge—nothing less than control of a large, strategic, and economically valuable portion of the known world. So for a long time neither opponent was willing to admit defeat. Thus, the war could be symbolized by two bleeding, exhausted boxers who struggle to stay on their feet, each hoping to land one last decisive punch and emerge the victor.

The Sicilian Crisis

Although the long-term cause of the war was the growing rivalry between Rome

and Carthage over control of the western Mediterranean, the immediate cause was in Sicily. The focus of the trouble was the Strait of Messina, which was vital to Roman interests. The Italian city of Rhegium faced the Sicilian city of Messina across this narrow channel. Rome, which now controlled all of southern Italy, needed unlimited, guaranteed access to the strait because it linked Italy's western ports with its eastern ones on the Adriatic Sea. The Adriatic, an inlet of the Mediterranean, separated Italy from Illyria, the sparsely populated lands northwest of Greece. Although Rome had no warships, it did have growing fleets of merchant ships. These vessels, many of them acquired during the recent conquest of the Italian Greek cities, sailed freely back and forth through the strait, expanding Roman sea trade.

In 265 King Hiero of Syracuse, the prosperous Sicilian Greek city located about seventy miles south of the strait, began a military expedition against Messina. A few years before, a band of pirates who called themselves the Sons of Mars had seized Messina, killed all the men, and enslaved the women and children. Since that time, the brigands had incessantly terrorized neighboring towns, some of them allies of Syracuse, and Hiero finally decided

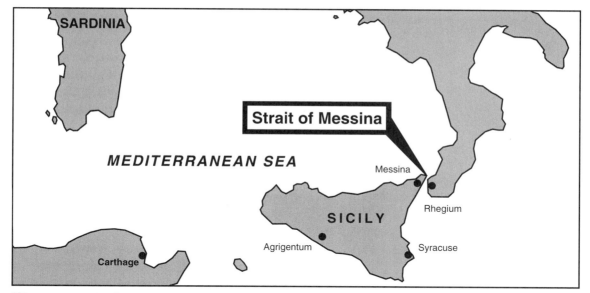

The narrow strait of Messina was Rome's crucial access corridor connecting the western and eastern Italian trading spheres.

to rid the region of this menace. While he was besieging Messina, some of the Sons of Mars appealed to Carthage for help. The Carthaginian Council was only too happy to respond, since it saw a chance to control the strategic strait and thereby ensure continued domination by Carthage of the western Mediterranean sea trade. The Carthaginians quickly sailed to Messina and seized much of the city, thus taking command of the strait.

The situation then rapidly became more complicated. One faction of the Sons of Mars, a group at odds with the contingent that had asked Carthage for aid, now appealed to the Romans. For Rome, the appeal was a mere formality. Roman leaders, already worried about Carthage's control of large stretches of the western and southern Sicilian coasts, viewed its rival's sudden command of the Messina strait as a serious threat to security. As Polybius put it, the Romans

were therefore in great apprehension lest, if [the Carthaginians] . . . became masters of Sicily, they would be most troublesome and dangerous neighbors, hemming them in on all sides and threatening every part of Italy. That they would soon be supreme in Sicily, if the [Sons of Mars] were not helped, was evident; for once Messina had fallen into their hands, they would shortly subdue Syracuse also, as [the Carthaginians] were absolute lords of almost all the rest of Sicily.[15]

For Rome, the Sicilian crisis was also a convenient excuse to launch the inevitable confrontation with Carthage. The Romans rationalized a military intervention in Sicily in two ways. First, they said, the "residents" of Messina had begged them for help. Second, by interfering in Messina's troubles, the Carthaginians had broken a long-standing agreement

Roman Siege Tactics

The Romans besieged Messina in 264 B.C. and in 261 did the same to Agrigentum, a Carthaginian stronghold in Sicily. Over time, the Romans became very adept in military siege tactics, employing many successful methods and devices, as scholars Anthony Marks and Graham Tingay explain in this excerpt from The Romans.

"The Romans were very determined fighters. They even conquered towns that were protected by high walls or built on clifftops. . . . First the Romans surrounded the town. Some soldiers tried to break holes in the walls. Others built siegeworks, wooden scaffolding and platforms that enabled them to climb the walls. If soldiers wanted to approach the wall without being hit by the enemy's arrows, they grouped together and covered themselves completely with their shields. This formation was called a *testudo* (tortoise). Large stationary crossbows were used to fire spears. Sometimes burning rags were attached to the tips. The *onager* was a larger, heavy catapult, capable of firing massive rocks over 500 meters (1,600 feet). Most effective of all were siege towers. They were taller than the city walls. . . . When finished, the siege tower was pushed up to the walls and soldiers climbed up inside. A drawbridge was lowered [from the tower's top] so that the soldiers could enter the city."

This carving depicts Roman legionnaires utilizing the protective testudo, *or tortoise, formation.*

between Rome and Carthage: in the late sixth century B.C., the two nations had signed a treaty in which they had agreed to stay out of each other's spheres of influence—Italy for the Romans and the western seas and islands for the Carthaginians. The parties had renewed the agreement about the year 348, and again, this time very halfheartedly, in 279. Now, in 264, claiming that the Strait of Messina was a part of its own sphere, Rome accused Carthage of violating the treaty and declared war. The death struggle between the two great powers had begun.

Roman Daring and Determination

At the beginning of the conflict, Rome's lack of war fleets constituted a definite disadvantage against a maritime power like Carthage. But the Romans did not seem worried. Apparently they felt confident that their land forces could dislodge the Carthaginians from Messina and that Carthage might then abandon Sicily.

At first, this confidence seemed well founded, for events went more or less in Rome's favor. Appius Claudius, one of the consuls serving in 264, marched an army south to Rhegium and had a meeting with Hanno, the commander of the Carthaginian forces at Messina. Hanno arrogantly warned Claudius to withdraw, bragging that Carthage's superior naval power could ward off any Roman attack. Unimpressed, Claudius ordered a daring night operation, in which hundreds of small merchant craft and fishing boats ferried Roman troops across the strait. The Romans immediately surrounded Messina

and besieged the city, forcing Hanno to retreat. Upon his return to Carthage, the defeated commander was promptly crucified. Meanwhile, the Romans continued their successful campaign in eastern Sicily. Syracuse's Hiero, who at first had allied himself with Carthage, wisely decided that the Romans were potentially the more formidable foe and switched sides. Thereafter, he remained a loyal ally of Rome.

Despite Rome's initial successes, however, within a few months it was surprised to find itself on the defensive. As the war dragged on, the naval superiority of Carthage increasingly became the deciding factor in the fighting. Carthaginian warships blockaded Sicilian ports, keeping Roman supplies from getting through, and Roman troops frequently suffered from hunger and lack of proper equipment. At the same time, Carthaginian fleets kept the African nation's outposts in Sicily well supplied. Eventually, after four years of largely indecisive fighting, the Romans grudgingly concluded that the only way to force the Carthaginians out of Sicily was to build their own fleets. In this endeavor, according to Polybius, the Romans' renowned resourcefulness and adaptability came to the fore:

As their shipwrights were absolutely inexperienced in building quinqueremes [large warships having five rowers at each oar], such ships never having been in use in Italy, the matter caused them much difficulty, and this fact shows us better than anything else how spirited and daring the Romans are when they are determined to do a thing. It was not that they had fairly good resources for it, but they had none whatever, nor had they ever given a thought to the sea; yet when they once had conceived the project, they took it in hand so boldly, that before gaining any experience in the matter they at once engaged [challenged] the Carthaginians who had held for generations undisputed command of the sea.[16]

The immediate problem the Romans faced was lack of knowledge about warship design and construction, coupled with lack of experienced crews to man any ships that could be built. Earlier, however, they had managed to capture a Carthaginian quinquereme. Roman engineers carefully dismantled the vessel, and an army of carpenters, using this design as a model, performed the incredible feat of building 140 warships in the brief span of sixty days. Meanwhile, thousands of soldiers, most of whom had never been on a ship, underwent a crash naval training program. "While trees were being cut down

and transformed with amazing speed into ships," comments Dorothy Mills, "benches were set up on the shore and day after day soldiers took their places on them and practiced rowing."[17]

The World's Greatest Sea Battles

The new Roman fleet was impressive. Each ship had three hundred oarsmen, who could propel the vessel to a speed of twelve miles per hour, which was fast enough to overtake an enemy ship or inflict serious damage by ramming it. At the time, sinking enemy warships by ramming them was the chief offensive naval strategy. Another common tactic was to draw near an enemy ship and throw spears, shoot flaming arrows, or catapult rocks at it. The Roman commanders correctly reasoned that simply having plenty of warships was not enough to en-

A Roman trireme, *or three-tiered warship, carried over 100 soldiers, as many as 300 oarsmen, and reached a maximum speed of 12 miles per hour.*

In the battle of Mylae in 260 B.C., a crow gangway holds a Roman ship and its Carthaginian prey together in a deadly embrace. The crows helped to ensure a Roman victory.

sure victory, since the Carthaginians were backed by centuries of experience in naval tactics. So the Romans searched desperately for an extra advantage.

They found this advantage in a new "secret weapon" called the *corvus*, or crow. The device consisted of a long wooden gangway, normally resting horizontally on a ship's deck, but capable of being raised to an upright position by ropes and pulleys. At the crucial moment in a battle, when the Roman captain maneuvered his vessel alongside an enemy ship, crewmen cut the ropes. The crow, which had a large metal spike protruding from the end, then crashed down onto the enemy deck, locking the two vessels together. At this point, some 120 sturdy and well-trained Roman legionnaires charged across the gangway and fought hand-to-hand with the enemy sailors.

The Romans were eager to test their new crow-equipped fleet. That fateful test came in 260 B.C. near Mylae, on Sicily's northeastern coast, in one of the largest sea battles ever fought anywhere up to

that time. According to the stunningly vivid account of Polybius, when the Roman commander, the consul Gaius Duilius, learned that the enemy was ravaging the area of Mylae,

he sailed against them with his whole force. The Carthaginians on sighting him put to sea . . . overjoyed and eager, as they despised [held in low esteem] the inexperience of the Romans. [The Carthaginians] all sailed straight on the enemy, not even thinking it worth while to maintain order in the attack. . . . On approaching and seeing the crows nodding aloft on the prow of each ship, the Carthaginians were at first nonplussed [confused], being surprised at the construction of the engines [devices]. However . . . the front ships attacked daringly. But when the ships that came into collision were in every case held fast by the machines [crows], and the Roman crews boarded by means of the crows and attacked them hand-to-hand on deck, some of the Carthaginians were cut

This engraving depicts the capture of part of a Carthaginian fleet by Roman warships. The loss of life in such close-fought naval battles was usually heavy.

down and others surrendered from dismay at what was happening, the battle having become just like a fight on land. So the first thirty [Carthaginian] ships . . . were taken [captured] with all their crews, including the commander's galley [vessel]. . . . The rest of the Carthaginian force . . . veered round the enemy . . . but when the crows swung round and plunged down in all directions . . . they finally gave way and took to flight, terror-stricken by this novel experience and with the loss of fifty ships.[18]

After their commanding victory at Mylae, the Romans engaged the Carthaginians in several more sea battles. Although the Romans generally held their own, they did not achieve clear-cut victories, mainly owing to the inexperience of their admirals. So the military advantage switched back and forth and the war remained largely indecisive. All the while, both sides lost large numbers of ships and men, which they quickly replaced at great expense. Finally, in 256 B.C., near Cape Ecnomus in south-central Sicily, the enemies clashed in the greatest naval battle of all ancient times. The Roman force had 330 huge warships and 140,000 men, compared to 350 ships and 150,000 men for the Carthaginian contingent. After a long and hotly contested fight, the Romans won, sinking over 30 enemy ships and capturing more than 60 others. The overall loss of life is unknown but likely exceeded 30,000.

The Romans Invade Africa

The victory at Cape Ecnomus seemed to give Rome the clear upper hand. The remnants of the main Carthaginian fleet having fled and dispersed, the northern African shore was now wide open to attack. Roman leaders reasoned correctly that all they had to do to win the war was launch a quick and decisive blow against Carthage itself. Wasting little time, in the summer of 256 the consul Marcus Regulus led the Roman armada southward and landed at Clupea, located on a peninsula about seventy-five miles east of Carthage. The Roman troops ravaged the peninsula, burning farms and estates, and easily defeating small Carthaginian units that tried to stop them. The overconfident members of Carthage's Council, believing their fleets invincible, had not adequately prepared for a direct invasion of their homeland. They had not taken such precautions as hiring a mercenary army to defend the

Double-Crossed by Carthage

Victory was not always sweet for the foreign mercenary leaders Carthage hired. The Carthaginian Council double-crossed the Greek general Xanthippus after he had saved Carthage by defeating the Roman consul Regulus in 255 B.C. In his Roman History, *the ancient Roman historian Appian describes the fates of the opposing leaders.*

"Not long after [the battle] the Carthaginians, weary of fighting, sent him [Regulus, who had been captured], in company with their own ambassadors, to Rome to obtain peace or to return if it were not granted. Yet Regulus in private urged the chief magistrates of Rome to continue the war with energy, and then went back [in Carthaginian custody] to certain torture; for the Carthaginians shut him up in a cage stuck full of spikes and thus put him to death. Xanthippus's success was the beginning of his ruin, for the Carthaginians, in order that the credit of such an exploit might not seem to be due to the Spartans [Xanthippus's countrymen], pretended to honor him with splendid gifts, and sent galleys to convey him back to Sparta, but [ordered] the captains of the ships to throw him and his Spartan comrades overboard. In this way he paid the penalty for his successes."

coastal cities and building extra defensive walls and outposts. It appeared to the Romans that a certain victory for Rome and the end of the war were in sight.

But as it turned out, the Romans were also guilty of overconfidence. Regulus was too slow to march on Carthage, the most strategic target, choosing instead to work his way methodically through the countryside. As the winter set in, the Roman Senate, worried that seasonal storms might damage their precious ships off the African coast, recalled some of the Roman forces. Regulus, now with a smaller army at his disposal, continued to delay, and in the meantime the Carthaginians took advantage of the situation. Their agents hurried to Greece, as the Picards explain,

> to recruit mercenaries. Normally they avoided applying to the [Greek generals for hire, since they] were expensive and had dangerous ambitions. These were not normal times, however, and the Carthaginians had to find soldiers capable of withstanding the [Roman] legions. . . . The agents found an officer of fortune named Xanthippus, a Spartan who had received excellent training in his country's war-schools. They engaged the Spartan as technical advisor. He soon reorganized the [Carthaginian] forces and explained their mistakes to the generals.[19]

Xanthippus quickly trained and drilled a combined force of mercenaries and native Carthaginians, creating a small but effective fighting unit of about twelve thousand infantry and four thousand cavalry. He also had about a hundred elephants. Boldly, in the spring of 255 B.C., he marched on Regulus's forces, which consisted of about fifteen thousand in-

fantry and five hundred cavalry. The armies clashed in the Bagradas Valley, southwest of Carthage, and Xanthippus's superior tactical abilities proved disastrous for the Romans. Describing the final moments of the battle, Polybius tells how the Greek phalanx outflanked and slaughtered the Roman troops. Of the surviving units,

> the greater number were trampled to death by the elephants, while the remainder were shot down by the numerous cavalry [wielding bows and arrows] in their ranks as they stood. Only quite a small body tried to effect their escape, and of these . . . some were dispatched by the elephants and cavalry, and about five hundred who got away with their general Regulus shortly afterwards fell into the enemy's hands and were made prisoners. . . . All the rest [of the Romans] perished.[20]

A String of Disasters

The overwhelming and embarrassing defeat in the Bagradas Valley was only the beginning of Rome's troubles. Hearing of Regulus's loss and capture, the Roman leaders sent a fleet to rescue the Roman survivors, but the Tunisian coast was now well guarded, and the attempt failed. As the fleet of more than 360 ships withdrew and sailed toward Sicily, a gigantic storm struck. Only eighty ships survived. "The rest," according to Polybius, "either foundered [sank] or were dashed by the waves against the rocks and headlands and broken to pieces, covering the shore with corpses and wreckage. History tells of no

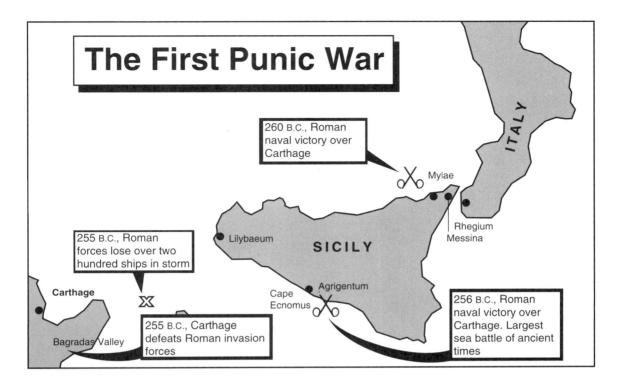

The First Punic War

260 B.C., Roman naval victory over Carthage

Mylae

ITALY

Rhegium
Messina

255 B.C., Roman forces lose over two hundred ships in storm

Lilybaeum

SICILY

Carthage

256 B.C., Roman naval victory over Carthage. Largest sea battle of ancient times

Cape Ecnomus

Agrigentum

Bagradas Valley

255 B.C., Carthage defeats Roman invasion forces

greater catastrophe at sea taking place at one time." [21]

Interviews with surviving ship captains indicated that the heavy crows on the warships' decks made the vessels top-heavy and therefore difficult to maneuver in heavy seas, contributing greatly to the scope of the disaster. But the stubborn Roman consuls and admirals were reluctant to give up the important offensive advantage of their unique naval device. The crows stayed, and the result was a string of new disasters. In the next few years, the Romans lost fleet after fleet in violent storms. Their casualties from storms alone in this first war with Carthage totaled more than seven hundred ships lost and over two hundred thousand sailors and legionnaires drowned. Because Rome constantly had to build new fleets and train new crews, the war dragged on and on.

During these years of prolonged and desperate fighting, which was once more centered around Sicily, the Romans had still another serious problem to deal with. The Carthaginian Council appointed a brilliant commander named Hamilcar Barca, known as the "man of lightning," to lead Carthage's forces. He was, says Gavin de Beer,

> endowed with a high degree of military genius. [He] perfected his well-trained army with promises of high pay, succeeded in stabilizing the [Carthaginian] position on land, and maintained a successful resistance in . . . the . . . positions which were still held by Carthage in Sicily, and which could be supplied by sea. [22]

Between 249 and 242 B.C., Hamilcar helped defeat Roman fleets and also conducted

Hamilcar Barca, Carthage's "man of lightning," whose son, Hannibal, would become Rome's most famous and hated nemesis.

frequent raids against Roman positions on the Italian and Sicilian coasts. Coastal towns lived in a state of constant fear that his ships might appear suddenly, burn and pillage homes and fields, and then escape just as quickly.

All or Nothing

After more than two decades of devastating battles and terrible losses of men, ships, and money, the Roman people were exhausted and the nation's treasury was empty. There was simply no more money left to build another fleet. By contrast, Carthage was still wealthy, its fleet had been replenished, and it had a formidable military leader in Hamilcar, who continued to harass and embarrass Roman commanders. The odds seemed heavily in Carthage's favor.

But the Romans were able to challenge these odds because they possessed a priceless human resource matched by few other peoples in history. This was their stern and renowned spirit of resolve in the face of hardship. Despite their horrendous losses, they refused to admit defeat. Ordinary Romans rescued the state, as by the thousands they contributed their own money, jewelry, and other valuables. The rich aristocrats, who normally hoarded their wealth, made the real difference, opening their pockets in an effort to create one last all-or-nothing fleet. "Owing to the patriotic and generous spirit of the leading citizens," says Polybius, "enough [money] was found to carry out the project; as either one, two, or three of them, according to their means, undertook to provide a quinquereme fully equipped. . . . In this way a fleet of two hundred quinqueremes [was] rapidly got ready."[23] This time, the Romans wisely constructed lighter vessels without crows, hoping to win by outmaneuvering the enemy.

This strategy paid off. Commanded by the consul Gaius Catulus, on March 10, 241 B.C., the new Roman fleet bravely attacked the Carthaginians near the Aegates Islands, off Sicily's western coast. Catulus won a major victory, sinking fifty enemy ships and capturing another seventy. The Carthaginian admiral, Hanno, who was unrelated to the Hanno who had lost Messina, escaped. But like his earlier namesake, he paid dearly for the defeat, dying on the cross soon afterward. With its fleet destroyed, Carthage could no longer supply its bases in Sicily, which meant that the island was lost. Moreover, the African coast once again lay unprotected. Rather than risk another Roman invasion of their homeland, the Carthaginians sued for peace.

While the atmosphere in Carthage must have been grim, in Rome it was just the opposite. Catulus entered the city in a magnificent victory triumph, during which his countrymen celebrated joyously. At a crucial moment in their history, they had gambled everything and won. Their defeat of the most powerful Mediterranean power brought not only personal satisfaction and heightened international prestige, but also the generous rewards of the treaty terms. The preliminary proposal presented to Carthage by Rome's negotiators, according to Polybius, was as follows:

> There shall be friendship between the Carthaginians and Romans on the following terms if approved by the Roman people. The Carthaginians [are] to evacuate the whole of Sicily and not to make war on Hiero or bear arms against the Syracusans . . . [and] to give up to the Romans all prisoners without ransom. The Carthaginians [are] to pay to the Romans by installments in twenty years 2,200 talents [the equivalent of millions of today's dollars].[24]

In fact, the Roman legislators did not approve the treaty in its preliminary form. They made the terms even harsher, reducing the payment period to ten years and increasing the penalty to thirty-two hundred talents, an enormous sum. In addition, Carthage was forbidden to sail its quinqueremes into any Roman waters. The Carthaginians were in no position to argue and reluctantly accepted the terms.

Thus ended the first great confrontation between the Mediterranean superpowers. In a way, Carthage got off lightly. Although it had lost its Sicilian possessions, it retained most of its empire, and

Carthaginian war vessels go down to defeat before the onslaught of a determined Roman fleet. After its victory in the First Punic War, Rome demanded and got heavy war reparations.

Into the Midst of the Enemy

In this excerpt from his Histories, *Polybius recounts some of the exploits of Carthage's "man of lightning," Hamilcar Barca, during the last few years of the First Punic War.*

"The Carthaginians . . . appointed Hamilcar surnamed Barca to the command [of Sicily] and entrusted naval operations to him. He started with the fleet to ravage the Italian coast . . . and after laying waste [to] Locris and Bruttii [at the tip of the Italian boot] quitted those parts and descended with his whole fleet on the territory of Panormus [in Sicily]. Here he seized on a place called Hercte . . . thought to possess peculiar advantages for the safe and prolonged stay of an army. . . . On the side looking to the sea and on that which faces the interior of the island, [the area] is surrounded by inaccessible cliffs. . . . Besides this Hercte commands a harbor very well situated for ships making the voyage from [Sicily] to Italy . . . and with an abundant supply of water. . . . Here Hamilcar established his quarters at great risk indeed, since he had neither the support of any of their own towns nor any prospect of support from elsewhere, but had thrown himself into the midst of the enemy. Notwithstanding this, the peril to which he put the Romans, and the combats to which he forced them, were by no means slight or insignificant. For in the first place he would sally out with his fleet from this place, and devastate the coast of Italy as far as Cumae [only 120 miles south of Rome], and next, after the Romans had taken up a position on land in front of the city of Panormus . . . he harassed them by delivering during almost three years constant and variously contrived attacks by land."

its major cities had escaped damage. Also, because of its mercenary military policy, it had lost far fewer native citizens in the fighting than Rome had. Moreover, the prospect of renewed peacetime trade was expected to result in the replenishing of Carthage's treasury and the restoration of its economy. That, after all, was the main concern of the empire's merchant rulers. However Hamilcar Barca, the chief military leader, had other ideas; he was consumed by a personal hatred for Rome and everything it stood for. The seeds of vengeance he soon began to sow would, in the fullness of time, produce a harvest of fear and death for millions.

3 Expansion by Naked Aggression: The Between-War Years

The two decades following the First Punic War were simultaneously turbulent and productive for both Rome and Carthage. Victory over Carthage gave the Romans a burst of confidence and energy, and they aggressively renewed the policy of economic and physical expansion they had pursued before the conflict. Now that they had complete control of Sicily, that expansion was aimed at areas beyond the Italian boot. The Carthaginians, with Hamilcar Barca still their chief military figure, also attempted revival and expansion. Having lost Sicily, they looked farther west for new territories and markets, in particular seeking to build a large power base in Spain.

It was during these years that Roman mistrust of Carthage and the corresponding Carthaginian hatred of Rome, especially by Hamilcar, manifested themselves. All the peoples of the Mediterranean sphere found it increasingly evident that the troubles between the region's two superpowers were far from over. Perhaps the most significant development during this period went largely unnoticed and unappreciated for a long time. This was the childhood, and subsequent rise to power over Carthage's armies, of Hamilcar's son Hannibal, one of the greatest military figures in world history. Possessing a unique personality, dynamic individual initiative,

and tactical genius, Hannibal became a driving force propelling the two nations toward another fateful and devastating collision.

Roman Imperialism

In the years immediately following the treaty signing, the thought of another devastating war was the last thing on the minds of most Roman and Carthaginian leaders. For Rome, the new era of peace was a time to reflect on the mistakes of the preceding conflict. Clearly, the republic had waited too long to become a naval power. That its consuls and other military officers had been novices in naval warfare had been another costly drawback. And time, ships, and men had been wasted in attempting, through the use of crows and large shipboard infantry units, to fight sea battles in the same manner as land battles. Roman leaders saw to it that these errors would not be repeated. From now on, Rome would maintain its naval power, put the fleets under the command of trained admirals, and build light, easily maneuverable warships.

Rome's new naval power seemed to give it almost unlimited opportunities for the future. In fact, this power, coupled

A fleet of Roman ships patrols western Mediterranean waters. After the first war with Carthage, Rome continuously maintained a strong and effective naval fighting force.

with the acquisition of Sicily, forever changed Rome's destiny as a nation. As James Breasted explains:

> For the first time she held territory outside of Italy, and from this step she was never able to withdraw. It has been compared with the action of the United States in taking Puerto Rico and the Philippines; for in gaining interests and responsibilities across the sea a nation is at once thrown into conflict with other powers having similar interests, and this conflict of interests never reaches an end, but easily and usually leads from one war to another.[25]

Thus, Rome's gains in the First Punic War whetted its appetite for further gains and launched its national policy of foreign imperialism, the drive to dominate and control other lands.

The first example of the new Roman imperialism occurred only three years after the conclusion of the war with Carthage. In 239 B.C., a group of former Carthaginian mercenaries living in Sardinia launched a rebellion against Carthage's local authorities on the island. The Carthaginians still controlled Sardinia and were well within their rights in suppressing the revolt. But when the rebels appealed to Rome for help, the Romans, in violation of the treaty they themselves had recently dictated to Carthage, decided to intervene. In 238, in a clear act of naked aggression, Rome annexed both Sardinia and Corsica. When the Carthaginian Council protested, the Romans threatened war; Carthage, in no position to enter another war, had no choice but to give up the islands. Adding insult to injury, Rome also increased the amount of the yearly indemnity Carthage was supposed to pay.

More examples of Roman aggression and expansion soon followed. Pirates based in Illyria had been harassing Roman and Greek shipping in the Adriatic Sea for some time. In 229 Rome sent a military expedition, which swiftly wiped out the pirates and at the same time established Roman domination over local Illyrian rulers. The Romans then set up a permanent military base in southern Illyria, just north of Epirus. Not long afterward, Rome expanded northward into the Po Valley. For centuries, this area, which the Romans called Cisalpine Gaul, had been inhabited by a hardy tribal folk—the Gauls. When, in the late 230s and early 220s, some of the Gallic tribes began raiding south of the Po River, the Romans saw an excuse to make a long-desired move on the Po Valley. Between 225 and 220, Rome defeated the Gauls and extended the power of the republic over all the northern Italian lands south of the Alps. Expansion into Sardinia, Corsica, Illyria, and Cisalpine Gaul not only increased Rome's territory and population, but also stimulated its economy by greatly enlarging the volume of its trade.

Mutiny of the Mercenaries

Meanwhile, Carthage desired to expand its own power, influence, and economy. But this was very difficult at first, partly because of its unjust and embarrassing loss

Demands for Roman Lands

One of the many political and social changes that occurred in Italy following the First Punic War was a demand for equitable land distribution by members of the increasingly powerful middle class. In this excerpt from his History of Rome, *noted classical historian Michael Grant explains.*

"This middle class included many men who, like the poor, were clients of [supported and voted as directed by] dominant noble patrons. Other members of this same intermediate category, however, were sufficiently independent to stand up, from time to time, for the underprivileged. Thus, on one notable occasion in the 230s they directly challenged the wishes of the nobility in the interests of those who were impoverished and landless. . . . Apart from the foundation of a Roman and a Latin colony [in one place or another], Rome had made extremely little use of its lands, initially because there had been no demand for them. Yet later the situation had changed, because the First Punic War produced ex-soldiers who had seen their farms gone to ruin while they were away on active service and who therefore demanded to be given new land to replace what they had lost. As a result, during the difficult decade that followed the conclusion of the Carthaginian war, there was intense popular pressure for breaking up the Ager Gallicus [former Gallic lands in northeast Italy] into small, individual allotments."

of Sardinia and Corsica to the Romans in 238. Also, the Roman indemnity, the original amount alone being equivalent to more than fifty tons of silver, was crippling. Though Carthage continued to engage in mercantile trade, its economy could not effectively revive until the war debt had been paid. Carthage tried to borrow the money in Egypt, but, unwilling to incur Rome's wrath, Egypt's rulers, the Ptolemies, refused.

In addition, Carthage had to contend with serious domestic troubles almost immediately after its defeat in the First Punic War. The worst of these was a direct result of the war debt, which had depleted the national treasury. Claiming poverty, the Carthaginian Council made the mistake of offering some of the mercenaries less money than Hamilcar had promised them. About twenty thousand of these hired soldiers mutinied, ravaged the Tunisian countryside, and marched on Carthage. Several local subject peoples, unhappy with Carthaginian rule, joined them. According to Polybius, the Carthaginians

> fell into a state of utter depression . . . things having turned out quite otherwise than they had expected. For they had been much worn by the long continued war for Sicily, and had hoped that the peace would procure them some rest and a grateful period of tranquility, and what happened was just the reverse, as they were now threatened by the outbreak of a greater and more formidable war. In the former case they were disputing the dominion of Sicily with the Romans, but now, with a civil war on their hands, they were about to fight for their own existence and that of their native city.[26]

In desperation, the city leaders summoned Hamilcar, who quickly rounded up all the loyal troops he could find—about ten thousand at most—and some seventy elephants. During 241–239 B.C., the period of this so-called Mercenary War, sometimes referred to as the "Truceless War," the fighting was bloody and both sides were guilty of terrible atrocities, or acts of inhumane cruelty. A typical example was the treatment of a group of Carthaginian prisoners by the mercenaries, as reported by Polybius: "After cutting off their hands they cut off the wretched [unfortunate] men's other extremities [sexual organs] too, and after thus mutilating them and breaking their legs, threw them still alive into a trench."[27] Though for a while Carthage seemed on the brink of ruin, Hamilcar's resourcefulness and military prowess saved the day. He repeatedly outsmarted and outmaneuvered the mutineers, winning several battles. Finally, in 239 he lured the last large force of mercenaries into a ravine. In the ensuing ambush Hamilcar's small army annihilated most of its opponents.

An Ideal Location for a Kingdom

Thanks to Hamilcar, Carthage remained intact. Its merchant rulers now looked forward to concentrating on business, paying off the war debt, and achieving new prosperity. But Hamilcar was not content merely to go about business as usual. He blamed the harsh Roman indemnity for the Mercenary War that had almost destroyed his country. He was also enraged, with justification, over Rome's outright

Hamilcar, with his small band of loyal veterans and his battle line of elephants, savagely annihilates the rebellious mercenaries in the "Truceless War."

theft of Sardinia and Corsica. Thus Hamilcar swore revenge on Rome, and though his long-range plans remain unclear, they almost certainly included an eventual resumption of hostilities. But to carry out such plans, Hamilcar realized, he had to have money, territory, armies, and abundant supplies. He also had to have a certain measure of autonomy, or independence, from the Carthaginian government, which might not endorse and support his personal policies. The Picards explain further:

In order to restore Carthage to her former greatness, and at the same time avenge her defeats, [Hamilcar] decided to turn once more to Spain. . . . For more than eight centuries the Phoenicians had been exploiting the resources of the Spanish peninsula, both economically and as regards manpower. . . . The Spanish [natives] had never been made to submit to political or military domination, however . . . [for] Carthage had felt no need to assume direct administrative control. . . . Hamilcar could no longer afford to [accept this] arrangement. . . . He wished, above all, to build up the necessary political and military power to enable him to carry out his plans. . . . The only way . . . [was] by founding

Spain Under Carthaginian Rule

Carthaginian rule of Spain between 237 and 219 B.C. by Hamilcar Barca and his relatives was authoritarian and harsh. In this tract from The Life and Death of Carthage, *scholars Gilbert and Colette Picard set the scene.*

"[Spain was then] a colonial state in which the native population was roughly treated and exploited. All positions of authority were in Carthaginian hands. The sovereign was advised by a Council [like the one in Carthage]. . . . The native princes were obliged not only to pay tribute [large sums of money], but to send one of their children, and even sometimes their wives, as hostages to New Carthage. Furthermore, they were closely watched by very active secret police, and those who were suspected of insubordination were under the constant threat of assassination, or else they disappeared and died amid terrible tortures and suffering. This was the fate of a [local] prince . . . who was later avenged by one of his followers assassinating Hasdrubal [in 221 B.C.]. Those in more modest circumstances were no better treated, and . . . a great number of peasants were reduced to serfdom [working the rulers' lands in exchange for a bed and food], while the workers in the mines were subject to extremely severe discipline. Indeed, the [Carthaginian] conquest caused the decline of the brilliant Iberian [Spanish] civilization, to which the Romans were [later] to deal the final blow."

one of those colonial and military monarchies which had grown up all around the eastern end of the Mediterranean. . . . These monarchies had been based on the power and doctrine of leadership, by which an adventurer at the head of a devoted army could appropriate for his own use the labor of a subdued population.[28]

Hamilcar identified Spain as an ideal location to build his own little kingdom, a base from which he might eventually oppose Rome. The Spanish peninsula seemed to be so far from Rome that the Romans would pay little attention to what he was doing, and also sufficiently removed from Carthage and his own political opponents. Even if these opponents objected to his actions, they lacked the resources to stop him at such a great distance and, after all, he reasoned, the projected kingdom in Spain was really in the best interest of Carthage.

In 237, therefore, Hamilcar took his army to Gades, the Carthaginian stronghold in southwestern Spain, and began his conquest of the peninsula. His gains were spectacular. In only a few years he subdued all the lands up to Cape Nao, almost halfway up the eastern coast of Spain. As he went along, he enlisted conquered Spanish natives as soldiers. He paid the new men well, and they became loyal and valuable military assets, making his growing army the best Carthage had ever possessed. At the same time, Hamilcar wisely sent back to Carthage a generous portion of the revenues he collected from Spain's rich silver mines. This gesture largely silenced his political opponents and ensured the mother city's continued support for his conquest.

During Hamilcar's conquests in Spain in the late 230s, his son Hannibal was a teenager. A brilliant and energetic young man, Hannibal learned all about military strategy and tactics from his father. He also absorbed his father's stubborn hatred of Rome and his desire for revenge. According to the ancient Roman historian Cornelius Nepos in his work *On the Great Generals of Foreign Nations*, Hannibal later said:

> My father Hamilcar, when I was a small boy not more than nine years old, just as he was setting out from Carthage to Spain . . . asked me if I would like to go with him on the campaign. I eagerly accepted. . . . Thereupon he said: "I will [take you] provided you will give me the pledge that I ask." With that he led me to an altar . . . [and] bade me lay hold of the altar and swear that I would never be a friend to the Romans. For my part, up to my present time of life, I have kept the

Young Hannibal, at his father's request, faithfully swears an oath never to trust or to make friends with the Romans.

oath which I swore to my father so faithfully.[29]

No doubt as Hannibal matured his father groomed him to help in the coming struggle with Rome. But Hamilcar's dreams of father-and-son conquest were cut short when he unexpectedly died in a drowning accident in 229. Since Hannibal was still too young to take command, Hamilcar's son-in-law, Hasdrubal, inherited control of Carthage's new Spanish holdings. Hasdrubal continued the conquest of Spain, pushing far into the hilly interior of the country. He also set up as his main base Carthago Nova, or New Carthage, along a magnificent harbor on the coast about seventy miles south of Cape Nao.

Keeping an Eye on Carthaginian Expansion

This activity did not go unnoticed in Rome. Contrary to Hamilcar's original expectations, the Romans did not consider Spain too far away to merit concern. In fact, they were very worried about Carthaginian expansion and kept a watchful eye on both Hamilcar's and Hasdrubal's gains. In an effort to ensure that Carthage would not extend its influence farther north into Europe, in 226 Rome "suggested" that Hasdrubal sign a special treaty. This document forbade the Carthaginians from crossing the Jucar River, about thirty miles north of Cape Nao. Feeling that the time was not yet right to take a stand against Rome, Hasdrubal signed the treaty. Also at about this time, the Romans made an alliance with the city-state of Saguntum, located about twenty miles north of the Jucar. This associ-

ation, Rome hoped, would help create a barrier to further Carthaginian expansion.

But Rome's efforts in this respect were ultimately in vain. In 221 Hasdrubal was murdered by a discontented Spanish native whose chief had been crucified by the Carthaginians. Hannibal, now twenty-six, succeeded Hasdrubal and, after having the assassin tortured and executed, took command of Carthage's Spanish kingdom. Though still relatively young, Hannibal, a skilled and inspiring leader with a remarkable and magnetic personality, had already earned the respect and devotion of his soldiers. Of his unique qualities, the first century B.C. Roman historian Livy tells us:

Never was the same nature more adaptable to things the most diverse—obedience and command. . . . When any bold or difficult deed was to be done, there was no one whom Hasdrubal liked better to entrust with it, nor did any other leader inspire his men with greater confidence or daring. To reckless courage in incurring dangers [Hannibal] united [combined] the greatest judgment [wise decisions] when in the midst of them. No toil could exhaust his body or overcome his spirit. Of heat and cold he was equally tolerant. . . . His times of waking and sleeping were not marked off by day or night: what time remained when his work was done he gave to sleep, which he did not court with a soft bed . . . but was seen repeatedly by many lying on the ground wrapped in a common soldier's cloak. . . . His dress was in no way superior to that of his fellows. . . . Both of horsemen and of foot-soldiers he

Hannibal (247–183 B.C.), one of the greatest military generals of the ancient world, initiated the Second Punic War by laying siege to the Spanish city of Saguntum, a Roman ally.

months and resulted in much misery, destruction, and loss of life. Describing the city's fall in 219, Appian wrote:

The Saguntines . . . when famine weighed heavily upon them, and Hannibal kept up the blockade [of relief supplies] without intermission . . . issued an edict to bring all the silver and gold, public and private, to the forum [main square], where they melted it down with lead and brass, so that it should be useless to Hannibal. Then, thinking it was better to die fighting than starve to death, they made a sally [advance] by night upon the lines of the besiegers while they were still asleep . . . and killed some as they were getting out of bed. . . . The battle continued until many of the Carthaginians and all the Saguntines were slain. When the [Saguntine] women witnessed the slaughter of their husbands from the walls, some of them threw themselves from the housetops, others hanged themselves, and others slew their children and then themselves. Such was the end of Saguntum, once a great and powerful city.[31]

Choosing War

Hearing of Saguntum's fall, the angry Romans sent ambassadors directly to Carthage. Their message was straight to the point—surrender Hannibal or face a new war with Rome. According to Appian, the chief Roman ambassador told the Carthaginian Council members, "Here, Carthaginians, I bring you peace or war, you may take whichever you choose." The legislators/rulers, upset over Roman meddling in

was undoubtedly the first [best]—foremost to enter battle, and last to leave it when the fighting had begun.[30]

Hannibal's ascendancy marked one of the great turning points in European history. He could have observed the terms of the treaty Hasdrubal had made with Rome, contenting himself with Carthage's new Spanish territories and riches. But like his father, Hamilcar, Hannibal hated the Romans and was anxious to make them pay for their past actions against Carthage. So in 220 B.C. he boldly violated the treaty by crossing the Jucar River and attacking Rome's ally, Saguntum. As the siege of the city began, the terrified Saguntines appealed to Rome for aid, and a delegation of Roman ambassadors sailed to Spain and demanded that Hannibal cease his hostilities. Not surprisingly, he rejected this demand. The siege of Saguntum lasted eight

The Wrong River

Polybius went into considerably more detail than other ancient historians about the meeting between the Carthaginian Council and the Roman ambassadors following the fall of Saguntum. His account in The Histories, *from which this excerpt comes, is very valuable, but he did make one mistake. He cited the Ebro, located some eighty miles north of Saguntum, rather than the Jucar, as the river in the treaty made between Rome and Hasdrubal in 226* B.C., *an error that misled many modern historians.*

"The Romans, on hearing of the calamity that had befallen Saguntum, at once appointed ambassadors and sent them post-haste to Carthage, giving the Carthaginians the option of two alternatives. . . . Either they must give up Hannibal . . . or war would be declared. [As] the Roman envoys . . . deliver[ed] their message the Carthaginians listened with indignation to this choice. . . . They said not a word of the treaty with Hasdrubal, considering it as not existent, or if existent, as not concerning them, since it was made without their approval. Here, they quoted . . . [from] the treaty made in the war for Sicily . . . in which they said there was no mention of Spain, but it was expressly set down that the allies of each power should be secure from attack by the other. They pointed out that at the time [of the earlier treaty] the Saguntines were not the allies of Rome, and to prove their point they read aloud several extracts from the treaty. . . .

I . . . will now give the reply of the Romans. . . . In the first place they contend[ed] that the treaty with Hasdrubal should not be ignored, as the Carthaginians had the audacity to say. . . . Hasdrubal [the Romans argued, had] . . . unconditionally made the agreement [in 226 B.C.] in which was the clause, 'The Carthaginians shall not cross the Ebro in arms.'. . . Therefore, if we take the destruction of Saguntum to be the cause of the war we must allow that the Carthaginians were in the wrong in beginning the war . . . in view of the convention made with Hasdrubal, by which the Carthaginians undertook not to cross the Ebro in arms."

their Spanish territories, refused to give up Hannibal. The Romans then threatened war again and the Carthaginians replied enthusiastically, "We accept it!"[32]

Upon the ambassadors' return to Italy, Rome promptly declared war, officially initiating the second great conflict between the two nations. As they had at the start of the first war, most Roman leaders assumed that victory would be attained fairly quickly and easily. Once more, they were dead wrong.

Chapter

4 Daring, Fortitude, and Genius: Hannibal Invades Italy

The seventeen-year-long conflict known as the Second Punic War was even larger in scope and more devastating than the first war between Rome and Carthage. Apparently the combatants had not learned their lesson, for once again each began the fateful enterprise believing it could achieve a relatively quick and decisive victory. Just as in the preceding struggle, this attitude proved to have been grossly over-confident. The new war became a long and costly battle for survival, a conflict that nearly destroyed an entire generation of Roman men and in which the fighting raged almost to the very walls of both mother cities.

It must be noted, however, that for one brief shining moment one side—Carthage—did hold a potential early and overwhelming victory within its grasp. This achievement was due to Hannibal's brilliant prosecution of the first phase of the war, lasting from 218 to 216 B.C. Hannibal began by shrewdly deducing his adversaries' initial strategy. From the Roman viewpoint, the Carthaginians represented a distant and therefore minimal threat. Although Hannibal had a large, well-trained army, he possessed no war fleets, which meant that he could not sail from Spain to Italy and attack Rome. If he tried marching his forces northeast toward Italy, he

would reach the towering, snow-covered Alps, which, the Romans believed, no army could safely cross. Thus, from the

Hannibal and his men prepare for their fateful journey over the Alps. Believing that no army could make it over the mountain barrier, the Romans did not expect this bold strategy.

Roman perspective, Italy was safe. Hannibal would surely hurry back to Tunisia to defend Carthage, on which Rome would launch a massive and successful attack.

A Bold Strategy

But the Romans did not yet realize that they were up against a man of great daring, fortitude, and genius. Defying the military logic of the time, Hannibal decided on a bold and unexpected strategy—to cross the Alps and march directly on Rome. His goal was to encourage and lead a rebellion of the various Italian peoples Rome had earlier subdued. Without their support, he believed, Rome would weaken and crumble. In one of the cleverest and most audacious military plans ever executed, Hannibal did succeed in surprising his opponents, who paid dearly for having underestimated him.

The first confirmation of the Carthaginian general's brilliance was that the Romans initially did exactly what Hannibal expected them to do. Shortly after Rome declared war, early in 218 B.C., Roman leaders began preparations for a two-pronged offensive against the enemy. One army would descend on Tunisia and besiege Carthage. Another Roman force would sail west, land in southern Gaul, and then march southwest and attack Hannibal's Spanish kingdom. To make his own plan work, Hannibal would have to get to southern Gaul and march toward the Alps before the Romans arrived.

Wasting no time, therefore, Hannibal set out from east-central Spain with foot soldiers and cavalry totaling perhaps forty to fifty thousand men, and also thirty-seven elephants. A few of the soldiers were Carthaginians but most were mercenaries from Numidia, Carthage's neighbor on the northeastern coast of Africa, and from Spain and Gaul. A large portion of the

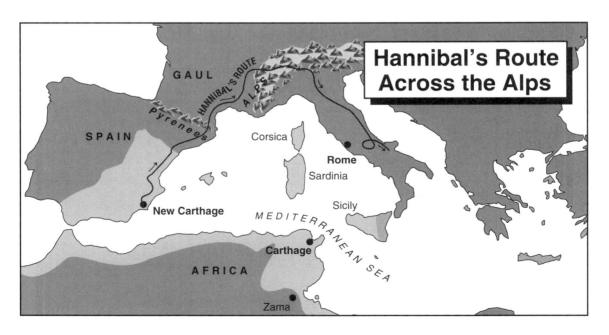

foot soldiers were heavy infantrymen who fought in full armor in a phalanx style similar to that utilized by Pyrrhus and other Greek generals. But the army included other important elements, as described by Gavin de Beer:

> In addition to the heavy infantry [was] light infantry; [consisting of] *peltasts* [spear throwers] . . . with light shields, and *psiloi* [club wielders] . . . with no armor. The most distinctive feature of Carthaginian infantry were the slingers, or Balearic Islanders, who were organized in corps of two thousand men, armed with two types of sling, one for long-distance fire and the other for close-quarters shooting. The missiles which they threw were stone pebbles or leaden bullets, and their accuracy was such that they could hit a hair set up as a target. Their fire-power was superior to that of the best contemporary archers. The cavalry consisted of heavy units, composed of Spaniards . . . and auxiliary squadrons of Gauls. The best troops of the Carthaginian army, however, were the Numidians. . . . The name Numidian means nomad, and they were born horsemen. Armed with a spear [to jab] and javelins [to throw], they were lightly clad, mounted on sturdy little horses, without saddles or bridles. . . . Endowed with phenomenal powers of endurance in man and horse . . . they were . . . the best light cavalry [in the known world].[33]

Hannibal knew that despite the fighting prowess of his own men, the Romans had at their disposal much larger forces, all well organized and highly trained. At the time, Rome's standing army alone consisted of about sixty-two thousand infantry and nearly four thousand cavalry. And the Romans could easily and quickly mobilize another fifty to sixty thousand infantry and thirty-five hundred cavalry in an emergency. Hannibal counted on the element of surprise and on the probability that Roman forces would be divided and scattered on several fronts.

Hannibal Crosses the Alps

Hannibal had a close call with one of the Roman forces in April 218 B.C. By this time, the Carthaginian had made it to the Rhone River, in southern Gaul, not far from foothills of the Alps. A Roman army had just landed near the river's mouth. The commander was the consul Publius Cornelius Scipio, who expected to march on Spain according to plan and did not realize at first that Hannibal was in the area. Incredibly, the opposing armies came within less than fifty miles of each other. When Scipio learned that Hannibal was nearby, he rushed to the attack, but found only the abandoned Carthaginian camp. The wily Hannibal had already moved on toward his first main objective—the Alps.

The Carthaginian crossing of the Alps was one of history's greatest feats of courage and physical endurance. Making it through the steep, ice-choked mountain passes would have been difficult and dangerous for a small group of individuals, let alone an army of men, horses, and elephants. The soldiers were understandably frightened. But Hannibal gathered them together and raised their spirits. The historian Livy offered a likely version of the general's pep talk:

Hannibal leads his army through the treacherous Alpine passes. Scholars still debate the exact route he took.

What do you imagine the Alps to be other than lofty mountains? Suppose them to be higher than the peaks of the Pyrenees [in northern Spain], but surely no region in the world can touch the sky or be impassable to man. Even the Alps are inhabited and cultivated, animals are bred and reared there, their gorges and ravines can be crossed by armies. What can be inaccessible to the soldier who carries nothing with him but his weapons of war? What toils and perils you went through for eight months to capture Saguntum! And now that Rome, the capital of the world, is your goal, can you deem anything so difficult or arduous that it should prevent you from reaching it?[34]

Delivering such morale-boosting speeches when he had to, Hannibal resolutely led his men through the Alpine passes. The journey was slow and painful. Often, huge rocks blocked the narrow pathways be-

tween peaks, fierce mountain tribes launched deadly ambushes, and men and animals slipped and fell hundreds or thousands of feet to their deaths. A vivid passage from *Punica*, an epic depiction of the Second Punic War by the ancient Roman writer Silius Italicus, gives some idea of the difficult passage.

[Hannibal] was the first to master [each new] height and from the crag's top called on his men to follow. Where the ascent was stiff with frozen ice and the slippery path over the snow-slopes baffled them, he cut steps with steel [spikes] in the resisting ice. When the snow thawed, it swallowed down the men in its opened jaws, and, as it rushed down from a height, buried whole companies beneath an avalanche. . . . The higher they climbed in their struggle to reach the top, the harder grew their toil. When one height had been mastered, a second opened and sprang up before their aching sight. . . . And as far as their eyes could reach, the same scene of frozen snow forced itself upon them. . . . And now, on top of the . . . difficulties of the ascent, half-savage men peeped out from the rocks, showing faces hideous with filth. . . . Pouring forth from caves in the hollow rock, the natives of the Alps attacked them. . . . Here, the snow turned red, deeply dyed with blood.[35]

The Sounds of Slaughter

After the grueling ordeal in the Alps, and more than five months after leaving Spain, Hannibal led his men at last into the green foothills of the Po Valley. His losses had been heavy. His forces now numbered only twenty thousand foot soldiers, six thousand cavalry, and a few elephants. But he was confident that in time the Roman

subject peoples would mutiny and swell his ranks.

In the meantime, Scipio, realizing that Hannibal was crossing the Alps, had sent his own army on to Spain, then rushed back to northern Italy. There, the consul assumed command of a second Roman army that was already on its way to stop Hannibal. The other consul, Tiberius Sempronius Longus, was in Sicily preparing to invade Africa with a third army when he received the shocking news that Hannibal had reached Italy. While Longus rushed his men northward, Scipio decided to go ahead and engage the enemy. In mid-December of 218 B.C., most of Hannibal's six thousand horsemen met a Roman cavalry force of about two thousand in a skirmish near the Ticinus River, a northern tributary of the Po. The Romans took heavy casualties, and Scipio himself was badly wounded. He would have been captured, too, had it not been for his son, of the same name, who led a small force

Having brought his men to the southeastern slopes of the Italian Alps, Hannibal triumphantly shows them their destination—the green hills and pastures of the fertile Po Valley.

directly into the Carthaginian ranks and made a rescue. After the Roman cavalry retreated, the main part of the army fell back to the south bank of the Po and waited for Longus to reinforce it.

In late December, the two Roman armies joined up, creating a total force of about forty-four thousand and, because of the elder Scipio's wounds, Longus assumed command. Rashly ignoring his colleague's warnings of caution, Longus mobilized his forces near the Trebia River, one of the Po's southern tributaries, and immediately fell into a clever trap Hanni-

A Dangerous Descent

In his History from the Founding of the City, *the great first century B.C. Roman historian Livy gives a detailed description of Hannibal's journey through the Alps in 218 B.C. In this excerpt, the Carthaginians and their animals struggle to climb down a steep and dangerous mountainside.*

"They then came to a much narrower cliff, and with rocks so perpendicular [vertical] that it was difficult for a . . . soldier to manage the descent, though he felt his way and clung with his hands to the bushes and roots that projected here and there. The place had been steep before, and a recent landslide had carried it away to a drop-off of a good thousand feet. . . . Then came a terrible struggle on the slippery surface, for it afforded them no foothold, while the downward slope made their feet the more quickly slide from under them; so that whether they tried to pull themselves up with their hands, or used their knees, these supports themselves would slip, and down they would come again! . . . The baggage animals, as they went over the snow, would sometimes . . . cut into the lowest crust, and pitching forward and striking out with their hoofs . . . would break clean through it, so that numbers of them were caught fast, as if entrapped, in the hard, deep-frozen snow. At last, when men and beasts had been worn out to no avail, they encamped upon the ridge. . . . The soldiers were then set to work to construct a road across the cliff—their only possible way. Since they had to cut through the rock, they felled some huge trees . . . and lopping off their branches, made an enormous pile of logs. This they set on fire . . . and pouring vinegar over the glowing rocks, caused them to crumble. After thus heating the crag with fire, they opened a [path]way in it with iron tools, and relieved the steepness of the cliff with zigzags of a more gentle slope, so that not only the baggage animals but even the elephants could be led down."

bal had engineered. Early one morning, before the Romans had eaten their breakfast, a force of Carthaginian cavalry approached the Roman camp. When Longus ordered his army out to meet them, the horsemen pretended to retreat and the Romans pursued, in the process wading chest-high in the river's icy, numbing waters. The Carthaginians were waiting on the other side of the river and the two armies crashed together. Unbeknownst to the Romans, who were already at a disadvantage because of hunger and numb limbs, Hannibal had hidden a force of Numidian cavalry behind a nearby hill. According to Polybius, the Numidians suddenly rode from their hiding place and

> attacked the enemy's center from the rear, upon which the whole Roman army was thrown into the utmost confusion and distress. At length both of [Longus's] wings, hard pressed in front by the elephants and all round their flanks by the light-armed troops, turned and were driven by their pursuers back on the river behind them. . . . The greater part were killed near the river . . . but [a] few infantry . . . escaped and most of the cavalry retreated.[36]

After this embarrassing defeat, the Romans fell back and spent the rest of the winter camped over a hundred miles south of the Po. Hannibal, meanwhile, wintered near the Trebia, where the cold killed some of his horses and all but one of the elephants.

But these losses were small compared to Hannibal's gains. His impressive victory at the Trebia convinced many Gauls to join his cause, and his army swelled to perhaps fifty thousand men. Eager to press his advantage, in the spring of 217 Hannibal marched his troops south to Lake Trasimene, only seventy miles north of Rome. There, in a great battle, he engaged the forces of a new consul, Gaius Flaminius Nepos, usually referred to simply as Flaminius, and once more engineered a brilliant ambush. Surrounded, the Romans fought bravely and desperately, but their situation was hopeless. The chaos and deafening sounds of the slaughter were so great that no one was aware that another disaster was happening at the same time. According to Plutarch, "At the very crisis of the battle, an earthquake occurred, by which cities were overthrown, rivers diverted from their channels, and fragments of cliffs torn away. And yet . . . not one of the combatants noticed it at all."[37] The defeat was the worst yet for Rome. The Carthaginians killed over fifteen thousand Romans, including the commander, Flaminius, and captured another fifteen thousand.

The Delayer

Hannibal, who had suffered very minimal losses at Lake Trasimene, was now in a strategic position to strike at the mighty symbol of his hated enemies—the city of Rome itself. But while more impetuous, inexperienced leaders might have jumped at this opportunity, Hannibal wisely refrained. For one thing, he reasoned, gaining control of such a large and well-fortified city would take a long time. During this interval his forces would be stationary and the Romans would surely raise new armies and surround him. Rome also had the advantage of its seaport of

Phantom Ships and Other Omens

The Romans, like many other ancient peoples, were very superstitious. They often regarded unusual happenings as omens, supernatural warnings that something of great importance, good or bad, was about to happen. Here, in his history of Rome, Livy lists the evil omens that supposedly preceded the disastrous Roman defeat at Lake Trasimene.

"In Rome or near it many prodigies [strange or marvelous events] occurred that winter, or—as often happens when men's thoughts are once turned upon religion—many were reported and too easily credited [believed]. Some of these portents [omens] were: that a free-born infant of six months had cried 'Triumph!' in the marketplace; that in the cattle market an ox had climbed, of its own accord, to the third story of a house, and then . . . had thrown itself down; that phantom ships had been seen gleaming in the sky . . . that in Lanuvium a slain victim had stirred, and a raven had flown into Juno's temple and landed on her very couch; that in the district of Amiternum, in many places apparitions [ghostlike images] of men in shining raiment [outfits] had appeared in the distance, but had not drawn near to anyone; that in the Picentian region [the region of Placentia] there had been a shower of pebbles . . . that in Gaul a wolf had snatched a sentry's sword from its scabbard and run off with it."

Ostia, near the mouth of the Tiber. Utilizing Ostia and the river, Roman fleets could keep the city well supplied indefinitely, and Hannibal, without ships of his own, would be powerless to stop them. Among the other important reasons for Hannibal's decision not to move directly on Rome, Michael Grant points out that

he lacked good siege equipment; and in its absence, the walls of Rome could not be breached by any attacker, especially without a supply base nearby. And no such base existed because, to Hannibal's acute disappointment, not one single town of central Italy defected to his side. Rome's system of

colonies and allies stood this searching test with admirable firmness.[38]

Thus, Hannibal swerved around Rome and moved into south-central Italy, hoping that there, finally, he could incite the revolt of Rome's subject peoples that was vital to his plan.

In the meantime, the Romans expected their enemy to attack Rome at any moment. In this dire emergency, the government appointed a "dictator," a trusted official given complete, although temporary, authority over the country. Chosen in the exercise of this rarely used power was Fabius Maximus, an aristocrat and military man with a reputation for honesty and sound judgment. According to Plutarch:

> The situation demanded a sole and absolute authority, which [the Romans] called a dictatorship, and a man who would wield this authority with energy and without fear. . . . Fabius Maximus, and he alone, was such a man, having a spirit and a dignity of character that fully matched the greatness of the office.[39]

Upon taking charge, Fabius immediately ordered the raising of new legions. He also destroyed the bridges leading to Rome and burned all the crops in the vicinity, to deny Hannibal the use of these valuable resources. When it became clear that the enemy had bypassed Rome and was heading south, Fabius embarked on a new and wise policy for dealing with Hannibal. This strategy, de Beer explains, was the reverse of that of Fabius's predecessors and

> a radical departure from what had previously been the Roman method of making war, which was to attack the enemy. After the disasters which the Roman army had just suffered at his hands, Fabius saw that Hannibal must not be given the chance to do what he most wanted, which was to fight pitched battles in open country. Fabius therefore kept his men in the foothills of the Apennines, where Hannibal's cavalry could not get at them, while he harassed Hannibal's foraging parties by guerrilla warfare. Hannibal tried every stratagem to taunt or coax Fabius into giving battle . . . but the old Roman stuck to his principles for which reason the Romans gave him the additional name of Cunctator, or Delayer.[40]

Using such delaying tactics, which have been called "Fabian" ever since, Fabius shadowed the Carthaginians as they marched through and pillaged south-central Italy.

Catastrophe at Cannae

But while Fabius's strategy was effective, many Romans began to criticize it. Often, Hannibal's soldiers ravaged fields and villages in plain sight of Roman legionnaires, who were forbidden by the dictator from interfering. Not surprisingly, when Fabius's six-month term as dictator ended, hotter heads vied for power in the consular elections of 216. The new consuls, Gaius Terentius Varro and Lucius Aemilius Paullus, with the blessing of the senators and most other government officials, reversed Fabius's policy. Taking charge of a new Roman army, perhaps sixty to seventy thousand strong, Varro and Paullus moved on Hannibal, who was camped at Cannae, a southern Italian town near the Adriatic Sea. Although Hannibal, with forty to forty-five thousand soldiers, was clearly outnumbered, he was thrilled at this chance for battle. He realized full well that he had several advantages: first, over half the Roman legionnaires were new recruits, and second, his opponent Varro not only was overconfident but had no real military training.

On August 2, 216 B.C., as the two armies met, Hannibal displayed his tactical genius by engineering one of the most stunning and complete victories in military history. According to Plutarch's account:

In the battle, Hannibal practiced a double strategy. In the first place, he took advantage of the ground to put the wind at his back. This wind came down like a fiery hurricane, and raised a huge cloud of dust . . . and drove it over the Carthaginian lines hard into the faces of the Romans, who turned away to avoid it, and so fell into confusion. In the second place . . . the sturdiest and most warlike part of his force he stationed on either side of the center, and manned the center itself with his poorest soldiers. . . . The center

Fabius's Wisdom and Valor

After the Punic Wars, later generations of Romans came to see Fabius Maximus as a great man whose wisdom in using delaying tactics had helped save Italy from destruction by Hannibal. In his Life of Fabius, *Plutarch vividly describes how, during the months that Fabius shadowed Hannibal, most Romans criticized the dictator's tactics and only the wily Carthaginian recognized his opponent's brilliance.*

"He [Fabius] put all his hopes of victory in himself, believing that Heaven bestowed success by reason of wisdom and valor, and turned his attentions to Hannibal. He did not purpose [intend] to fight out the issue with him, but wished . . . to wear out and consume gradually [Hannibal's] great energies, his scanty resources, and his small army. Therefore, always pitching his camp in hilly regions so as to be out of the reach of the enemy's cavalry, he hung threateningly over them. If they sat still, he too kept quiet; but if they moved, he would ride his men down from the heights and show himself just far enough away to avoid being forced to fight . . . and yet near enough to make his very delays inspire the enemy with the fear that he was going to give battle at last. But for merely consuming time in this way he was generally despised by his countrymen, and roundly abused even in his own camp. Much more did his enemies think him a man of no courage and a mere nobody—all except Hannibal. He, and he alone, comprehended the cleverness of his opponent, and the style of warfare which he had adopted. He therefore made up his mind that by every possible device . . . his foe must be induced to fight, or else the Carthaginians were undone. . . . He resorted to every species of strategic trick and artifice, and tried them all, seeking, like a clever athlete, to get a hold upon his adversary. . . . But the purpose of Fabius . . . remained constant and unchangeable."

gave way and was followed by the Romans in pursuit, Hannibal's line of battle thus changing its shape into that of a crescent; and . . . the picked troops on his wings wheeled . . . swiftly to left and right and fell upon the exposed sides of their enemy, all of whom, except those who retired [retreated] before they were surrounded, were then overwhelmed and destroyed.[41]

The defeat at Cannae was the worst single military catastrophe in Roman history. Over fifty thousand Romans were slain, including the consul Paullus and some eighty senators, while Hannibal lost only six thousand men. Fear gripped the city of Rome, for it now seemed certain that Hannibal would move on the capital. But it stands as a monument to the courage and tenacity of the Roman people that in this, their darkest hour, no one considered the idea of surrender. Maintaining their fighting spirit, the Romans rallied around the defeated consul Varro when, with his head hung low, he returned to the city. As Livy reports:

In that very hour there was such courage in the hearts of the citizens that when the consul was returning from that defeat for which he himself had been chiefly responsible, a crowd of all sorts and conditions went out to meet him . . . and gave him thanks be-

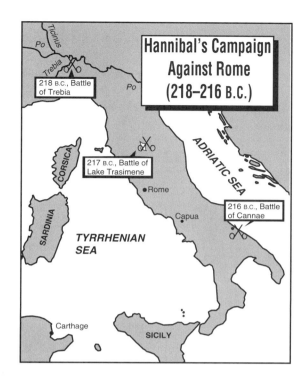

cause he had not despaired of [deserted] the state.[42]

Preparing for the worst, city officials armed criminals and slaves, and ordinary citizens set up makeshift workshops to construct weapons. There was no question in anyone's mind that Romans of all walks of life would defend their city and republic to the last man and woman. But when would the dreaded Hannibal launch his attack? This question had no such easy answer.

Chapter

5 Rome's Unbroken Spirit: The Tide of Battle Slowly Turns

After dealing the Romans a crippling defeat at Cannae in 216 B.C., Hannibal seemed to be on the brink of total victory. His army of war-hardened veterans was largely intact, while for the moment scarcely more than twenty thousand Roman soldiers were left in arms in all of Italy. There might not ever be a more opportune moment to strike hard and fast at the Roman capital. But once more, much to the surprise of the Romans themselves, Hannibal decided against attacking Rome. This prompted the famous remark by his cavalry commander: "In very truth the gods bestow not on the same man all their gifts; you know how to gain a victory, Hannibal: you know not how to use one."[43]

But Hannibal knew better. He still had no ships, no siege equipment, and no large permanent supply bases in Rome's vicinity, factors that made besieging Rome a risky if not foolhardy venture. So he chose instead to remain in southern Italy. His plan was to continue pillaging the countryside, defeating the Romans whenever he could, and wait for the Roman subject peoples to come to his side. And indeed, not long after Cannae, some did. Many of the former Samnite towns joined him, as did the important and prosperous city of Capua in

Hannibal's troops regularly ravaged the Italian countryside, killing Roman citizens, pillaging villages, and helping themselves to farmers' crops.

central Italy, about one hundred miles southeast of Rome. Hannibal hoped these defections would be the beginning of a great anti-Roman insurrection.

Thus, Hannibal's strategy was to wear down the Romans slowly and deliberately. As for the Romans, after Cannae they decided that Fabius had been right and returned to a strategy of delaying tactics, hoping to exhaust Hannibal before he exhausted them. As a result, the struggle over Italy dragged on for twelve more grueling years. During this second phase of the war, much fighting also took place outside of Italy, particularly in Sicily and Spain. Hannibal became increasingly frustrated, partly because he had no way of controlling or affecting these faraway battles. His worries also grew as the Romans, demonstrating their tremendous courage, endurance, and resilience, slowly recovered from their terrible losses.

Losses Outweighed by Advantages?

Rome's losses had been so damaging, in fact, that in the months following the Cannae disaster a full Roman recovery was far from assured. As Dorothy Mills describes the situation in late 216 B.C. and early 215 B.C.,

> The Roman resources were steadily growing less. The losses in battle had been so great that soon Rome would find it difficult to raise [new] armies; every available man was already in camp, and all the work at home was being done by women; the fairest parts of Italy had been laid waste [by Hannibal]; food was scarce and prices high;

Rome was suffering from all the evils which war brings in its train. Her spirit might remain unbroken to the end and her men die fighting heroically to the last, but without resources the day would have to come when she would perish, and the name of Rome remain only a memory.[44]

But the Romans possessed several unique advantages, both human and material, which allowed them to continue resisting and made a long-term recovery at least possible. Not the least of these advantages was their ability to bounce back from terrible suffering and hardships. They had demonstrated this courageous quality on a number of occasions—for example, when they built the fleet that won for them the First Punic War. Knowing that they were now defending their native land against a foreign invader made them even more willing to endure hardships. Second, Italy was a large and fertile country with many natural resources. Although Hannibal had destroyed numerous farms and crops, these could be replaced over time. What is more, Roman fleets controlled the seas around Italy, as well as its many rivers, which meant that the Romans could ship in supplies from elsewhere. Third, in the face of disaster Romans of all social classes joined ranks and supported the state with both loyalty and money. According to the Roman historian Lucius Florus in his *Epitome of Roman History*, when, after Cannae, Rome's treasury was empty,

> the senators voluntarily offered their wealth to the state. . . . The example of the Senate was followed by the knights [well-to-do military officers], who, in their turn, were imitated by the tribes [common people], with the result that

Capua Pays the Penalty

When in 211 B.C. the Romans captured Capua, which had joined Hannibal, they set an example to other towns that might consider deserting Rome by dealing harshly with the Capuans. Here, from his book Hannibal: One Man Against Rome, *historian Harold Lamb describes what happened after Capua surrendered.*

"The capital city of *Magna Graecia* was cut off and without means of withstanding the steady approach of the Roman siege works. There was bitter debate in its senate on the last day, before envoys went out to ask for terms of surrender. Some of the nobles hoped for leniency from the other Senate on the Tiber [that is, in the city of Rome]; most of them had no such hope. One of these, Vibius Virrius, declared that only one liberty was left them—to prepare their bodies in a fitting way for burning before the entrance of the Roman legion. . . . [After Virrius and twenty-seven other senators had poisoned themselves], the first legion marched into the gate. . . . Sentries were posted, and all weapons collected. . . . Capuans of senatorial rank were taken out to the quarters of the proconsuls [Roman leaders], who sentenced 53 to execution, the others to be sold as slaves. The *quaestors* [financial administrators] of the Roman camp collected together 2,070 pounds of gold and 33,200 pounds of silver from the homes of the captives. The balance of the citizens were sent into exile, and the city itself condemned to lose self-rule. . . . So Capua, like Syracuse, paid the penalty for taking arms against the Senate and the Roman people."

when . . . the resources of private individuals were poured into the public treasury, the registers and the hands of the clerks scarcely sufficed to record them [fast enough].[45]

Another long-term advantage the Romans possessed was their strong grip on conquered peoples, now their allies. Although Capua and several other southern Italian towns went over to Hannibal, many others did not. Almost all of northern Italy remained loyal, as did the majority of former Greek cities in the south, partly because of the Greeks' traditional hatred of the Carthaginians. The Romans also set an early example of what they would do to the disloyal. In 211 they besieged and retook Capua, publicly whipped and then beheaded the city's leaders, and enslaved the rest of the inhabitants. Capua's fate stood as a grim warning to other Italian towns that might contemplate joining Hannibal.

Rome Fights a King and a Genius

But Rome also had to contend with Hannibal's gaining of allies outside Italy. After this superb general's impressive show at Cannae, several foreign powers, reasoning that Carthage would likely win the war, scrambled to align themselves with Hannibal. Among these was Macedonia, the powerful kingdom that at the time encompassed most of Greece. In 215 B.C. the Macedonian king, Philip V, made an alliance with Hannibal, promising to aid the Carthaginian cause by attacking southwestern Italy. When the Romans learned of this alliance, they mustered a fleet under the command of Marcus Valerius Laevinus. In 214 Laevinus beat Philip to the punch by sailing across the Adriatic to the Illyrian city of Apollonia, where the Macedonian invasion force was assembling, defeating Philip, and burning his fleet. This launched the First Macedonian War, a subconflict of the larger war with Carthage, which would pit Rome against Philip for the next nine years.

Shortly after hostilities with the Macedonians began in 214, trouble erupted in Sicily, specifically Syracuse. Rome's old ally, Hiero, had recently died and his successors now allied themselves with Hannibal. Since Syracuse was still the most powerful city in Sicily, its anti-Roman stance posed a threat to the whole island, which was important to Rome strategically and as a source of food and other supplies. In 213, therefore, the Romans began a siege of Syracuse. The Roman commander, Marcus Claudius Marcellus, attacked the city both from land and from the sea. His naval strategy was to sail his ships up to the city walls, which di-

rectly bordered the harbor, and raise *sambucae*, large siege ladders on which Roman legionnaires might climb to the tops of the battlements.

But Marcellus's attempt at an early victory was foiled by the genius of a single Syracusan. He was Archimedes, a brilliant scientist who had studied at the renowned Greek university in Alexandria, Egypt, known as the Museum. Archimedes designed a series of ingenious weapons and mechanical devices with which to defend the city. Among these were catapults that could shoot projectiles farther and more

Archimedes of Syracuse (ca. 298–212 B.C.), the greatest mathematician and inventor of ancient times. Among his inventions was "Archimedes' screw," a rotating device that pumped water out of a river or lake.

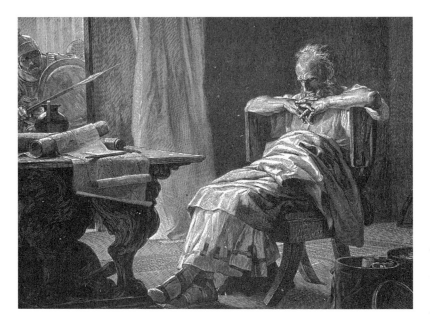

Lost in thought, Archimedes contemplates a mathematical problem as the Romans sack the city around him. A Roman soldier, unaware of the old man's identity, prepares to kill him.

accurately than any others yet invented and a huge lens that focused the sun's rays on the Roman ships, setting them ablaze. He also engineered a system of small holes in the city walls, through which the Syracusan defenders shot arrows and other missiles at approaching troops. Perhaps Archimedes' most amazing achievement was his design of huge mechanical cranes that extended far over the battlements and were capable of lifting whole warships out of the water. According to Polybius:

> These machines let down an iron hand [hook assembly] attached to a chain with which the man who piloted the beam would clutch at the ship, and when he had got hold of her by the prow [front] . . . [lifted] up the ship's prow [and] made her stand upright on her stern . . . and by means of a rope and pulley let the chain and hand suddenly drop from it. The result was that some of the vessels fell on

their sides, some entirely capsized, while the greater number, when their prows were thus dropped from a height, went under water and filled.[46]

Thanks to Archimedes, the siege dragged on for months. But though frustrated, Marcellus had only the greatest respect for Archimedes, and even joked about his own losses at the inventor's hands. "Archimedes uses my ships to ladle seawater into his wine cups," said Marcellus, comparing the siege to a great feast, "but my *sambuca* band is flogged out of the banquet in disgrace."[47] Anxious to meet Archimedes and hoping to persuade him to work for Rome, Marcellus, during his eventual capture of Syracuse in 212, gave orders that the scientist was not to be harmed. However, a Roman soldier who did not recognize Archimedes killed him, and thereby the world lost a mind that might have launched an industrial revolution two thousand years before the invention of the steam engine.

The Scipios in Spain

While the Romans fought the Macedonians and Syracusans, they also had to deal with the Carthaginian kingdom in Spain. From the beginning, Roman leaders had recognized the necessity of maintaining a military front in Spain. Hannibal's brother, Hasdrubal Barca, an able general in his own right, commanded this large power base, which had the capacity to keep Hannibal well reinforced with men and supplies. Indeed, the senior Scipio had sent his army on into Spain in 218 B.C. precisely to prevent this contingency.

After recovering from the wounds he had received at the Ticinus River, Scipio journeyed to Spain and, with his brother Gnaeus, took charge of the Spanish

The Wrath of Heaven

During the long siege of Syracuse, a sudden outburst of disease struck Syracusans and Romans alike, and many died on both sides. The ravages of the plague, of unknown identity, were vividly captured in this tract from Punica, *by the ancient Roman writer Silius Italicus.*

"The dogs were first to feel the mischief; next the birds flagged in their flight and dropped down from the black clouds; and then the beasts of the forest were laid low. Soon, the infernal plague spread further, depopulating the [Roman] camp and devouring the soldiers. Their tongues were parched; a cold sweat issued from the vital parts [organs] and poured down the shivering frame [body]; and the dry throat refused a passage to the nourishment prescribed [by doctors]. The lungs were shaken by a hard cough, and the breath of the thirsting sufferers came forth from their panting mouths as hot as fire. The sunken eyes could hardly endure the burden of light; the nose fell in; matter mixed with blood was vomited, and the wasted body was mere skin and bone. . . . The healing art was baffled by the disease. The ashes of the dead were heaped up till they formed a great pile. And all around lay corpses, unattended and unburied, for men feared to touch the infectious limbs. The deadly plague, growing by what it fed on, spread further and shook the walls of Syracuse with mourning as grievous [as that of the Romans] and made the [defenders] suffer no less than the Roman army. The wrath of heaven fell with equal destruction upon both sides, and the same image of death was present everywhere."

campaign. For several years, the brothers were successful. After stationing troops in the eastern foothills of the Pyrenees to keep Hasdrubal from marching into Gaul, they moved slowly down the coast, taking town after town until in 211 they captured Saguntum, the city whose siege by Hannibal had ignited the war. That same year, however, they met with military and personal disaster. Carthage sent massive reinforcements to Spain, tipping the balance against the Romans. In a bloody battle, the consul Scipio was defeated and killed along with most of his men, and in a separate engagement soon afterward Gnaeus met defeat and death at the hands of Hasdrubal's army. The Carthaginians then recaptured all the lands south of the Ebro River. They might have moved farther north had it not been for a courageous and brilliant young Roman officer, Lucius Marcius, who marshaled the remaining Roman forces and kept the enemy at bay.

A few months later, Rome sent reinforcements and a new commander—the younger Scipio, now twenty-five—who had lost both his father and his uncle and was eager to avenge their deaths. Scipio quickly regained much of the territory recently lost and then marched on New Carthage, the enemy's main stronghold. After his men had besieged and scaled the city's walls in 209 B.C., Scipio dealt harshly with the defenders. As Polybius tells it:

> The Romans, having once taken the wall, at first marched along it sweeping the enemy off it. . . . Upon reaching the gate some of [the Romans] descended and began to cut through the bolts, after which those outside began to force their way in. . . . When Scipio thought that a sufficient number of troops had entered he sent most of them . . . against the inhabitants of the city with orders to kill all they encountered, sparing none, and not to start

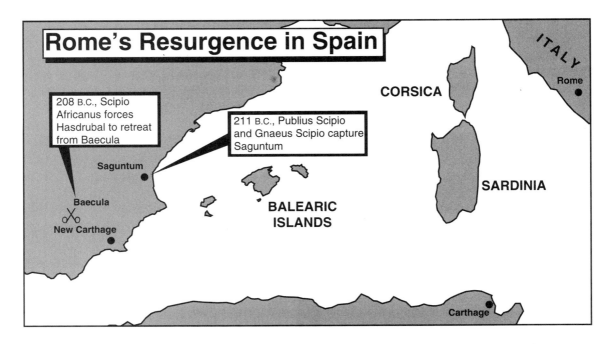

Rome's Resurgence in Spain

208 B.C., Scipio Africanus forces Hasdrubal to retreat from Baecula

211 B.C., Publius Scipio and Gnaeus Scipio capture Saguntum

ITALY
Rome
CORSICA
SARDINIA
Saguntum
Baecula
New Carthage
BALEARIC ISLANDS
Carthage

pillaging until the signal was given. The Romans do this, I think, to inspire terror, so that when towns are taken . . . one may often see not only the corpses of human beings, but dogs cut in half, and the dismembered limbs of other animals, and on this occasion such scenes were very many.[48]

The next year, following up his success at New Carthage, Scipio marched into central Spain. There, near the town of Baecula, he attacked Hasdrubal's army. Scipio had carefully studied Hannibal's tactics in Italy and now used some of them against the great general's brother, who wisely retreated after sustaining moderate losses. Not long afterward, while Scipio prepared to pursue the enemy and finish the job, Hasdrubal and his army escaped from Spain. According to Michael Grant, Hasdrubal took

> an unexpected land route around the western [and unguarded] extremity of the Pyrenees and [proceeded] on to Italy, with the intention of joining his brother there. His escape transformed the battle of Baecula from a tactical victory into a strategic defeat. And Scipio did not try to pursue him. . . . If he had done so, he would have exposed himself [to attack] in difficult country too far from his base and would thus have risked losing Spain altogether; and besides, he would never have caught Hasdrubal Barca in any case.[49]

Fateful Meeting at the Metaurus

Indeed, Hasdrubal drove his men hard and made it through Gaul faster than his brother had. Crossing the Alps in milder weather and by an easier route than Hannibal had selected, Hasdrubal descended into the Po Valley in 207 B.C. Counting some immediate defections of local Gauls to his ranks, his forces numbered about thirty thousand. The appearance of a second formidable Carthaginian army in Italy shocked and troubled the war-weary Romans. By this time, most of the loyal Italian towns were exhausted, unable to supply the state with any more troops or money, and Rome had all it could do to maintain its many existing war fronts. A coordinated attack on the homeland by the armies of Hannibal and Hasdrubal might spell a disastrous end for the republic.

At this dangerous and crucial moment, the desperate Romans had an unexpected stroke of good luck. Roman soldiers out foraging for food in southern Italy, not far from the region in which Hannibal was camped, noticed some travelers who seemed to be lost. When it became clear that the strangers were Carthaginians, the soldiers captured them and brought them before the local governor. "At first they tried to confuse him by vague answers," says Livy, "but when the fear of torture was brought to bear and compelled them to admit the truth, they informed him that they were carrying a letter from Hasdrubal to Hannibal."[50] The letter detailed a plan in which the two brothers would march northward and southward, respectively, meet near the Metaurus River, in northeastern Italy, and then assault Rome.

On acquiring this vital information, the consul Gaius Claudius Nero, whose army had been shadowing Hannibal, initiated a bold emergency plan. Leaving the bulk of his forces to guard Hannibal, Nero picked seven thousand of his best troops and led them on a rapid forced march northward. According to the plan, he would join forces with a larger army commanded by Marcus Livius and together they would surprise Hasdrubal. Livy's account captures the desperate northward march of Nero's men, slowed only by the crowds of well-wishers who cheered them along the way:

> They were marching everywhere between lines of men and women who had poured out from the farms on every side, and amidst their . . . prayers and words of praise. Defenders of the state men called them, champions of the city of Rome. . . . In their weapons and right hands, they said, were placed their own safety and freedom, and those of their children. . . . The soldiers competed in self-restraint. . . . There was no loitering, no straggling, no halt except while taking food; they marched day and night.[51]

As Nero had hoped, he and Livius took Hasdrubal completely by surprise. Confronted by the Romans near the Metaurus, the Carthaginian prepared his forces for battle, while Livius impressed on his own men the serious and crucial nature of the battle they were about to fight. "Look here, soldiers!" he roared. "Watch me as I rush into battle! Fill with your bodies the passage I open with my sword. . . . If we fail to overthrow their ranks with a speedy victory, and if Hannibal, the thunderbolt of Carthage, appears with his own army, what gods can save a single one of us from the horrors of hell below?"[52]

When the battle was joined, both sides fought furiously and valiantly, but the tide turned against the Carthaginians. As he saw his men being slaughtered and the battle lost, Hasdrubal chose death over capture. "When fortune unquestionably was on the enemy's side," Livy reports, "he spurred his horse and charged into a Roman unit. There, in a manner worthy of his father, Hamilcar, and of Hannibal his brother, he fell fighting."[53] Because most of Hasdrubal's troops met the same fate that day, it later became a popular saying that the battle at the Metaurus was Carthage's Cannae.

The Romans Rebound

In fact, the Roman victory at the Metaurus proved to be the great turning point of

Publius Cornelius Scipio, who later became known as Scipio Africanus, gained fame fighting in Spain before squaring off against the mighty Hannibal.

Spain Forever Lost

Scipio, the son of the Roman consul, who was later awarded the surname Africanus, was profoundly influenced by Hannibal's brilliant battlefield maneuvers. Employing many of his opponent's ideas, as well as some of his own, the Roman general reformed his army's usual tactics in preparation for the battle of Ilipa in 206 B.C. in southern Spain. The opposing forces were led by Hasdrubal, son of Gisgo, who had inherited command of Carthaginian Spain when Hasdrubal Barca had marched on Italy. In this excerpt from his book Scipio Africanus: Soldier and Politician, *classical scholar H. H. Scullard describes the fateful encounter.*

"As soon as it began to be light [Scipio] ordered his men to eat, arm themselves and march out of camp. This they did, and Scipio then launched his cavalry and light-armed troops against the enemy's camp. . . . The attack . . . accomplished its aim, since the Carthaginians hardly had time to arm themselves, and Hasdrubal was forced to lead out his men before they could take their morning meal. He at once dispatched his cavalry and light infantry against those of the enemy, and hastily drew up his heavy infantry on the plain near the foot of the hill. . . . The Romans remained inactive for a time, waiting until the Carthaginians began to feel their lack of nourishment and were further fatigued by standing in the heat of the day. The sun rose higher and higher while the cavalry engagement and skirmishers surged to and fro. At last, about noon, Scipio felt the time for action had come. He . . . advanced to within half a mile of the enemy. He then ordered his center of Spanish allies to continue their advances slowly, while he himself commanded the right wing, and Lucius Marcius . . . the left. . . . The Carthaginian elephants, which were placed in front of the two wings, became frightened and stampeded, harming their own side as much as the Romans. The superior training and ability of the Roman troops on the wings soon told against the Spaniards opposed to them. The latter put up a gallant fight, but were worn out by the heat of the day and lack of food. . . . So the Carthaginian wings gradually retreated, till they reached the foot of the hill, where they evidently hoped to make a stand, but when the Romans pushed their attack home they fled in disorder. . . . At last the struggle was terminated by a cloud-burst which forced the Romans to return to their camp. . . . Ilipa was the justification of Scipio's military reforms and methods, and of his whole policy: by it the fate of Spain was sealed and the Carthaginian cause there forever lost."

the war. The Romans had finally beaten the enemy in pitched battle on Italian soil. And in the process, they had eliminated Hannibal's best and last hope for reinforcement. The great general himself knew nothing of Hasdrubal's defeat until a few days after the battle, when a Roman soldier ran up to the Carthaginian camp and tossed in a blood-soaked sack. Inside was a human head, which Hannibal recognized as his brother's. According to ancient sources, a great sorrow came over Hannibal, not only for the loss of Hasdrubal, but because he knew that now the Carthaginian cause was also lost. Sadly, he marched his army into a remote region of the southern Apennines, where he remained in seclusion for the next four years.

Hannibal had once more demonstrated his great ability to grasp the essence of a military situation. Everywhere the Romans enthusiastically rebounded and triumphed. In 206 B.C. Scipio wiped out the last Carthaginian Spanish army in a bloody battle at Ilipa, in southern Spain, and Carthage's Spanish kingdom collapsed. The following year, the Romans signed a treaty with Philip of Macedonia, who had long since lost the stomach to fight Rome. The Romans could now concentrate all their resources on bringing the devastating war to a swift conclusion. Wisely, Roman leaders decided for the moment to bypass Hannibal and strike at a more strategic target. In a righteous fury over the near annihilation of an entire generation of Roman warriors, they would bring their desire for vengeance to the enemy's homeland. There the fate of the two nations would be decided once and for all before the battlements of Carthage itself.

Chapter

6 Death at the Door: The Second War's Bloody Climax

Between 205 and 204 B.C., the character of the Second Punic War changed radically. For more than a decade the Romans had fought the Carthaginians in Italy and on fronts stretching from Illyria in the east to Spain in the west. During all these years, while battles raged in Italy, Spain, and other lands, the Carthaginian homeland in northern Africa had remained largely untouched. Trying to maintain multiple war fronts, Rome had simply lacked the resources to mount an invasion of Carthage, as well. With Spain and Sicily firmly in Roman hands and Hannibal in hiding in the southern Italian mountains, however, the Romans were able to reallocate their resources. Thus, in the war's third and final stage, which lasted about three years, Carthage at last became the main focus of military operations. With his homeland in jeopardy, Hannibal could not stand idly by. He finally abandoned Italy and, in the war's dramatic and bloody climax, faced the Romans on the dusty plains of Tunisia.

Scipio Gets His Way

While Hannibal remained Carthage's principal military leader in the final phase of the war, Scipio emerged as Rome's main military figure. After wresting Spain from Carthage in 206 B.C., Scipio returned to Rome in a blaze of glory. In 205 he easily won election as consul and immediately proposed that Rome carry the war to Africa. This was not a new idea. Many earlier Roman generals had longed to open a front in Tunisia but had lacked the troops and supplies needed for such an ambitious operation. Even though Rome now had the necessary troops and supplies, however, Scipio encountered considerable opposition to his plan. Many senators and other political figures, including Hannibal's old nemesis Fabius Maximus, argued that Hannibal might still pose a dangerous threat in Italy. It would be wiser, they said, to defeat Hannibal once and for all and then invade Africa, rather than to divide Roman forces now.

But after numerous debates, both public and private, and a great deal of political wheeling and dealing, Scipio got his way. Late in 205, he established his initial base of operations in Sicily, where he trained his army and collected troop transports and warships. In the spring of 204, with a force of thirty thousand men carried on four hundred transports and forty warships, Scipio set sail from the Sicilian port of Lilybaeum. Two days later,

Scipio Africanus (seated) led the Roman invasion of the Carthaginian heartland in 204 B.C. At the time, he was perhaps the only living general who was a potential match for Hannibal.

he landed near Utica, only twenty-five miles northwest of Carthage. The immediate plan was to lay siege to Utica, in order to gain a foothold in the country and to secure the use of a good harbor.

While attacking Utica, Scipio considered his long-range plans. His own military situation was clearly favorable: both numerically and strategically, he was better off than the enemy. The Carthaginians had few local allies, the main exception being Syphax, a Numidian chief who had married the daughter of a Carthaginian aristocrat. Syphax helped Hasdrubal Gisgo, whom Scipio had earlier defeated at the battle of Ilipa in Spain, to raise a local army to oppose the Roman invaders. But the forces of Hasdrubal and Syphax were few in number and poorly trained.

By contrast, in addition to his own large and well-trained army, Scipio had a local ally—Masinissa, another Numidian leader—who hated Syphax and the Carthaginians and had been fighting both for some time. A brilliant and colorful character, Masinissa commanded a formi-

dable and renowned cavalry unit. Ancient sources differed on its size, describing it as numbering between six thousand and twenty thousand. But all agreed on how Masinissa used it effectively to wage guerrilla warfare on his enemies. According to Appian, for instance:

> Syphax and the Carthaginians were much the more numerous, but they marched with wagons and a great load of luggage and luxuries. On the other hand, Masinissa was an example, in every toil and hardship, and had only cavalry, no pack animals and no provisions. Thus he was able early to retreat, to attack, and to take refuge in strongholds. Even when he was overtaken, he often divided his forces so that they might scatter as best they could, concealing himself with a handful [of horsemen] until they should all come together again, by day or by night, at an appointed rendezvous. . . . Thus his enemies never could make a regular assault upon him, but were always warding off his attacks.[54]

While in Spain, Scipio had wisely made an alliance with Masinissa, who promised to help Rome against Carthage in the event of a Roman invasion of Africa.

Siege and Pillage

Now, that invasion was a reality, and Masinissa kept his word. While the siege and blockade of Utica continued, he and Scipio launched their first combined assault on Hasdrubal and Syphax. Scipio sent spies dressed as local servants into the enemy ranks and received reports that the Carthaginians' discipline was poor and their camp badly guarded. In a night attack on this camp, Mesinissa's mounted men galloped in and set the enemy tents and huts on fire. In the great chaos and confusion that resulted, Scipio's legionnaires entered the camp and slaughtered almost everyone in it. Syphax and Hasdrubal escaped and somehow managed to raise another small army, partly consisting of Spanish and Greek mercenaries. When Scipio and Masinissa easily defeated this new force, which was as untrained and badly disciplined as the last, Hasdrubal fled to Carthage. Syphax ran for Numidia, where Masinissa eventually captured him.

Filled with Admiration

Scipio and Masinissa, the Numidian cavalry commander, became allies in Spain in 206 B.C. when the Roman general was concluding his anti-Carthaginian campaign there. This excerpt from Livy's Roman history, in which the two leaders meet for the first time, reveals both Scipio's physical appearance and Masinissa's high regard for him.

"The Numidian had already been filled with admiration for [Scipio] in consequence of his reported achievements, and had conjured up in his mind an ideal figure, tall and stately. But greater still was the reverence he felt for the man in his presence; and while Scipio had great natural dignity, [his] long hair added charm, as did [his] general appearance . . . truly masculine and soldierly, and . . . at the height of physical strength. . . . Almost dazed by merely meeting him, the Numidian . . . was eager to give such services to Scipio and the Roman people that no individual foreigner would have aided the Roman state with more eagerness. That aid, although he had long wished to give it, he had been unable to furnish in Spain, a foreign and unknown land. But in the land in which he had been born and brought up in the hope of inheriting his father's kingdom, he would easily furnish it. If indeed the Romans should send Scipio as commander into Africa as well, he was quite confident that Carthage would be short-lived."

Scipio now pressed the siege of Utica with renewed vigor. The task was difficult, for the city had massive fortifications and was well defended. The efforts on both sides were captured dramatically in this tract by Appian, based on eyewitness accounts:

> Scipio besieged Utica by land and sea. He built a tower on two galleys joined together, from which he hurled missiles three cubits [five feet] long, and also great stones, at the enemy. He inflicted much damage and also suffered much, the ships being badly shattered. On the landward side he built great mounds, battered the wall with rams whenever he could get up to it, and tore off with hooks what hides and other coverings were on it. The enemy, on the other hand, undermined the mounds, turned the hooks aside with slip-knots, and deadened the force of the rams by dropping beams upon them crosswise. They also made sallies against the [siege] machines with fire whenever the wind was blowing toward them.[55]

Eventually, reasoning that the siege was wasting too much time and Roman energy, Scipio abandoned the operation. He then pursued a different strategy in which he pillaged the countryside around Carthage, attempting to disrupt the city's food supply, perhaps in preparation for an eventual attack on the Carthaginian capital.

At this juncture, with its local armies defeated and the Romans threatening to bring death to Carthage's very door, the desperate Carthaginian Council did two things. First, it sent word for Hannibal to return from Italy. Then it initiated peace negotiations with Scipio. Whether the sec-ond action was sincere or merely a ploy designed to give Hannibal time to cross to Africa and defend the city will never be known for sure. In any case, Hannibal landed at Leptis, over one hundred miles down the coast from Carthage, in the autumn of 203, and the Council suddenly rejected the idea of a peace treaty.

Hannibal's Lament

For Hannibal, the return to his homeland was in many ways a bitter one. Total victory had once seemed almost within his grasp and now he had to leave Italy, his crusade to destroy Rome a failure. In his view, his own countrymen were much to blame for this failure. During his long invasion of Italy, Carthaginian leaders had repeatedly refused to send him substantial reinforcements, choosing unwisely instead to fortify Spain. Thus, it is not surprising that Hannibal's reaction to being recalled was the angry remark, "The conqueror of Hannibal is . . . not the Roman people, so often cut to pieces and put to flight, but the Carthaginian senate."[56] Yet Hannibal did not abandon his country in its hour of need. Reluctantly, he gathered his forces, now numbering slightly more than twenty thousand, marched to the Italian coast, and commandeered some boats. Because Carthage had sent him no troop transports, he barely had room for his men and none at all for his magnificent cavalry horses, which, to keep the Romans from utilizing them, he killed. This made him sadder and more bitter than ever. Supposedly he even began to second-guess some of his own past moves in Italy. Livy continues:

They say that rarely has any other man leaving his country to go into exile departed so sorrowfully as Hannibal on withdrawing from the enemy's land; that he repeatedly looked back upon the shores of Italy and, accusing gods and men, called down a curse upon himself also . . . because he had not led his soldiers blood-stained from the victory at Cannae to [the conquest of] Rome. . . . Such were his . . . laments as he was dragged away from his long occupation of Italy.[57]

While Carthaginian leaders were relieved at Hannibal's return, Scipio was downright delighted. He had always dreamed of the possibility of squaring off against the man he rightly viewed as the world's greatest living military leader. Scipio knew that he himself would eventually get the glory for defeating Carthage on its own soil. Would not that glory be all the greater if he could defeat Hannibal in the process? Thus, the remainder of the war became, in essence, a personal battle between the two most formidable generals of the day.

Taking Each Other's Measure

At first, Hannibal and Scipio waged battle from a distance. For months each tried to outguess the other and to jockey for the best possible position from which to launch an attack. All the while, the two took advantage of the time to build up their respective forces. Scipio sent an urgent message to Masinissa, who was completing the conquest of Syphax's kingdom, asking him to return and help fight Hannibal. Meanwhile, Hannibal re-

A bust depicts Hannibal. On the plain of Zama, he led Carthage's last-ditch effort to repel the Roman invasion forces and avoid defeat.

cruited as many soldiers as he could, including a small contingent of Numidians still loyal to Syphax.

Eventually, in the spring of 202 B.C., the two armies camped several miles apart on the plain of Zama, about seventy-five miles southwest of Carthage. Each force consisted of about forty thousand infantry and cavalry, and Hannibal also had some eighty elephants. The two leaders, both confident and arrogant men, now tried to take each other's measure, and to this end Hannibal sent three spies to scout the Roman camp. The results of this mission were quite unexpected. In the narration of Polybius,

When these men were caught and brought before him, Scipio was so far from punishing them, as is the usual practice, that on the contrary he ordered a tribune to attend them and point out clearly to them the exact arrangement of the camp. After this had been done he asked them if the officer had explained everything to them with proper diligence. When they answered that he had done so, he furnished them with provisions and an escort, and told them to report carefully to Hannibal what had happened to them.[58]

Clearly, Scipio intended to show Hannibal that the Romans feared him so little that they cared not if he knew their strength and camp layout. Impressed with this psychological move designed to hurt Carthaginian morale, Hannibal desired to meet his daring and impudent adversary face-to-face. The two had not seen each other before, their only close encounter having been long ago in the cavalry skirmish at the Ticinus in which Scipio, then a young man, had rescued his father. When Hannibal proposed a meeting, Scipio eagerly accepted.

Describing this unique and fateful encounter, Livy says, "Keeping their armed men at the same distance the generals, each attended by one interpreter, met. . . . For a moment they remained silent, looking at each other and almost dumbfounded by mutual admiration." Then the two men spoke at some length. Although several ancient writers attempted to reconstruct the conversation, its actual content remains unknown. Evidently the two leaders could not reach any meaningful agreement, for as Livy continues, "Without

An artist's version of the legendary meeting between Hannibal and Scipio on the eve of the Zama battle.

making peace they returned from the conference to their armies, reporting that words had been of no avail; that arms must decide the issue and they must accept whatever lot the gods should give them."[59]

The Battle of Zama

The next day, the Roman and Carthaginian armies approached each other, and the final engagement of the long war took place. According to Appian's account:

Hannibal first ordered the trumpets [signaling the charge] to sound, and

Scipio responded in like manner. The elephants began the fight decked out in fearful battle array and urged on . . . by their riders. But [Masinissa's] Numidian horsemen, flying around them, incessantly thrust darts into them, until being wounded and put to flight and having become unmanageable, their riders took them out of the combat. . . . The field being cleared of these beasts the battle was now waged by men and horses only. The Roman right wing . . . put the opposing Numidians to flight and Masinissa struck down their prince, Massathes. . . . Hannibal, after rallying his left wing . . . [brought] up at the same time his second line of Carthaginians and Africans. Scipio, perceiving this, moved parallel to him with another body of troops. When the two greatest generals of the world thus met . . . there was . . . no lack of zeal on either side, the two armies fighting and cheering vehemently and keenly.[60]

Overall, the battle proceeded in clearcut stages. After the departure of the elephants, the Roman cavalry put the enemy horsemen to flight and Masinissa and his men gave chase, leaving the infantry behind on the field. Hannibal's front line, composed mainly of mercenaries and new recruits, was badly mauled by the Roman legionnaires and fell back. Hannibal then brought up his second line, made up of his formidable Italian veterans. These were a match for the Romans, but Scipio took the precaution of lengthening his own line to prevent the enemy from enveloping his wings as they had done to the

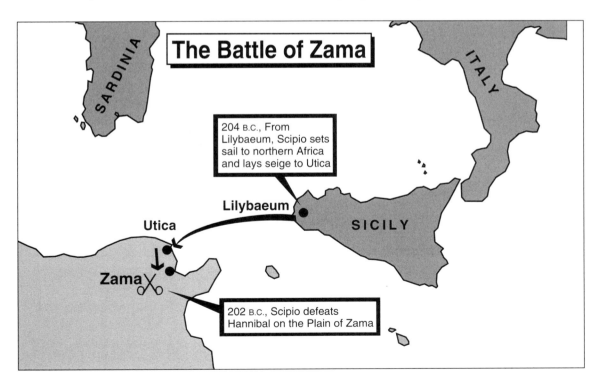

The Battle of Zama

204 B.C., From Lilybaeum, Scipio sets sail to northern Africa and lays seige to Utica

202 B.C., Scipio defeats Hannibal on the Plain of Zama

SARDINIA

ITALY

Lilybaeum

Utica

SICILY

Zama

Romans at Cannae. Eventually, Masinissa reappeared and, following Scipio's plan, performed this very maneuver: he swung his cavalry around the Carthaginian wings and attacked Hannibal's army from the rear. Thus the originator of this brilliant move suddenly found himself on the receiving end. Scipio's forces closed in from all sides and proceeded to annihilate the enemy. The slaughter was so great, Polybius later wrote, that the Romans were hampered by "the quantity of slippery corpses which were still soaked in blood and had fallen in heaps and the number of arms thrown away haphazard."[61]

For the first time in his legendary career, the great Hannibal had tasted defeat. In all, at least twenty thousand of his men died that day and most of the others were captured. With only a handful of men, the Carthaginian general escaped to the eastern Tunisian town of Hadrumetum. Roman casualties, by comparison, were relatively light, numbering probably between two thousand and four thousand. Clearly, after this crushing defeat Carthage

Brothers Joined in Death

Many legends grew up about the battles of the Second Punic War, and later Roman historians and writers often assumed they were factual. For example, in his Punica, *Silius Italicus cited an improbable episode of hand-to-hand combat on the field of Zama. This tale of the Roman brothers Herius and Pleminius confronting Hannibal himself is so personalized and romanticized that it is doubtful the author could have documented it as a real event.*

"Herius, who bore a noble name from the famous town of Teate . . . was aiming a thrust with his spear, when Hannibal at once rushed before him and prevented him. Herius, eager to meet a foe so famous, made a mighty effort; but Hannibal drove his sword up to the hilt in the Roman's body. The dying man's eyes sought his brother, Pleminius; and up Pleminius came. Maddened by his brother's fate, he brandished his sword in Hannibal's face, and with loud threats demanded the life of the dead man. Hannibal replied thus: 'Agreed, if you indeed are prepared to restore *my* brother to me! Only our bargain must be kept, and you must call back Hasdrubal from the shades [underworld]—Shall I ever forget the fierce hatred that I bear to Rome? Or shall I suffer my heart to be softened? Shall I spare a single son of Italy?'. . . Speaking thus he brought down the full weight of his shield upon Pleminius and felled him, where the earth, slippery with his brother's blood, made his footing insecure; then he attacked him with the sword. As Pleminius fell, he stretched out his hands to embrace the body of Herius; and the pangs of death were lightened because they died together."

The Carthaginian elephants charge at the Romans in the first phase of the fighting at Zama. The huge animals proved largely ineffective and the battle was decided by infantry and cavalry.

had no more credible means of resistance. The long, devastating war was over at last.

Rome's Triumph; Carthage's Punishment

When the news of total victory reached Rome, large and jubilant celebrations erupted everywhere. Upon landing in Italy, Scipio, now a national hero, was greeted by gigantic crowds, all cheering him loudly. He and his men entered Rome in the most magnificent victory triumph in the city's history. According to Appian:

> All who were in the procession wore crowns. Trumpeters led the advance . . . [followed by] wagons laden with spoils. Towers were borne along representing the captured cities, and pictures [huge drawings] showing the exploits of the war. . . . White oxen came next, and after them elephants and the captive Carthaginian and Numidian chiefs. Lictors [officers bearing Roman insignia] clad in purple tunics

preceded the general; also a chorus of harpists and pipers . . . and they marched in regular order, keeping step with song and dance. Next came a number of incense-bearers, and after them the general himself on a chariot embellished with various designs, wearing a crown of gold and precious stones, and dressed . . . in a purple toga interwoven with golden stars. . . . Riding in the same chariot with him were boys and girls, and on the horses on either side of him young men, his own relatives. . . . After these came the army, arranged in squadrons and cohorts, all of them crowned and wearing laurel branches.[62]

In recognition of his exploits in Africa, the Romans bestowed on Scipio the name "Africanus," by which he was known ever after.

By contrast, the mood in Carthage was far from cheerful, but this was understandable after the loss of the second great conflict with Rome. Although the city of Carthage itself had once more escaped destruction, the peace terms proposed by

Rome seemed a harsh punishment. The Carthaginians were to give up all claim to Spain and to their Mediterranean island possessions; surrender all their elephants; recognize Masinissa as the king of Numidia and an ally of Rome; pay an annual war indemnity of two hundred talents for a period of fifty years; give up all but ten of their warships, the remaining five hundred to be burned; and finally, pledge not to wage war against anyone without Roman permission. When Roman ambassadors presented these terms to the Carthaginian Council, Hannibal himself was present. He expressed the opinion that the terms were not nearly as harsh as they might have been and urged his countrymen to accept the treaty, which they did.

Many people on both sides were surprised that the surrender of Hannibal to Rome was not among the peace terms. Scipio, who so greatly admired his adversary, had made sure that the great general would be spared. This was also a wise political move. At the time, Hannibal was the only Carthaginian leader strong enough to keep the state intact and marginally prosperous and thereby to ensure that the war indemnity would be paid regularly.

In time, however, the Romans felt that Hannibal had accomplished this task too well. By 195 B.C., Carthage had revived many of its old trade routes and was financially sound. Worried, the Romans decided to remove Hannibal after all and to this end accused him of secretly collaborating with Rome's enemies. This charge was almost certainly false, for Hannibal had learned the hard way that Rome had become too powerful to challenge. Unwilling to submit to the indignity of capture, he fled to the eastern Mediterranean, where Roman agents pursued him from

country to country over the course of more than a decade. Meanwhile, hoping to remain in Rome's good graces, his own countrymen declared him an outlaw. Finally, in 183, with Roman agents closing in on him, Hannibal committed suicide by drinking poison. He was in his mid-sixties. Reportedly, his last words were, "Let us now put an end to the great anxiety of the Romans, who have thought it too lengthy, and too heavy a task, to wait for the death of a hated old man."[63]

Endurance and Discipline Win the Day

Ironically, Hannibal's former nemesis, Scipio Africanus, died that same year, also re-

Rejected by his countrymen and cornered far from home by Roman assassins, the great Hannibal commits suicide by drinking poison.

The Greatest Commanders

As Livy recounts in his Roman history, Scipio once asked Hannibal whom he considered to be the greatest commander in the world.

"'Alexander [the Great of Macedonia],' was the reply. [Scipio] Africanus then asked whom he would put second, and Hannibal replied, 'Pyrrhus.' On Scipio's again asking whom he regarded as the third, Hannibal, without hesitation, answered, 'Myself.' Scipio smiled and asked, 'What would you say if you had vanquished me?' 'In that case,' replied Hannibal, 'I should say that I surpassed Alexander and Pyrrhus, and all other commanders in the world.'"

jected by his countrymen. Years after the war's end, Scipio's political opponents had accused him of negotiating the treaty with Carthage to his own advantage and of stealing public monies. The charges were false, but the general's reputation had been tarnished beyond repair. He went into seclusion and ordered that his tombstone bear the words, "My ungrateful country shall not have my bones."[64] Scipio died believing that without him Rome could not have won the war.

Yet no single person had been responsible for the Roman victory over Carthage. It was instead a triumph of the Roman people's dogged determination and of the Roman state's solid and methodical organization. As Michael Grant puts it:

Victory had only been won by feats of unprecedented endurance. In spite of initial disastrous defeats, the Italian dominion built up with such patience by Rome had, on the whole, resisted the temptation to defect, fully justifying the Roman system. Even in the greatest peril Roman . . . morale and discipline had stood firm. . . . The solid virtues of many Romans and Italians, working together as loyal, obedient partners within a tradition built up over many generations, had prevailed and won the day.[65]

But passage of this supreme test of national endurance had also increased Rome's thirst for power and solidified the popular belief that the republic was destined to rule others. Over time, the strangle-cord of a widening Roman imperialism would claim many victims. But none would suffer so horribly and completely as Carthage, when, for the third and last time, it felt the fury of Rome's wrath.

7 Carthage in Flames: The Last Days of a Great City

The immediate result of the Roman victory in the Second Punic War was that Rome became the undisputed master of the western Mediterranean world. In addition to Italy and Sicily, Rome now completely controlled Illyria, the islands of Sardinia and Corsica, southern Gaul, and Spain. And with Carthage defeated and Numidia a staunch Roman ally, Rome's influence was supreme in most of northern Africa.

But these impressive gains represented only the beginning of Roman imperialism. Rome now turned its attention eastward toward Greece and the Middle East, where large Greek-ruled kingdoms held sway. The closest of these, King Philip's Macedonia, which had earlier dared to help Hannibal, was the first to feel the cold thrust of Roman steel. In 200 B.C., Scipio Africanus led a large military expedition to Greece and in just three years subdued the Macedonian kingdom. Not long after the conclusion of this so-called Second Macedonian War, Rome turned on the Seleucid kingdom, which encompassed Syria, Palestine, and other parts of the Middle East. By 190 the Romans had defeated the Seleucid king, Antiochus III. And by 167 Rome was in control of the last great Greek-ruled kingdom, the Ptolemaic, composed principally of Egypt. Rome transformed all these lands into vas-

sal states, which could manage their own affairs as long as they supported Rome and did its bidding.

"Carthage Must Be Destroyed"

In the meantime, Carthage watched uneasily as the entire Mediterranean became, in effect, a Roman lake. The Carthaginians were helpless to intervene because their loss in the Second Punic War had reduced them to a third-rate power struggling to survive in a world dominated by Rome. For decades, Carthage carefully honored the terms of the treaty. It built no more warships, refrained from making war on anyone, and in general did Rome's bidding. But this was not enough for many Romans, who still saw Carthage as a potential threat. The Romans had almost always dealt leniently with conquered peoples, but their hatred and distrust of Carthage ran deep. Eventually deciding to eliminate the Carthaginian threat once and for all, in 149 B.C. Rome launched the Third Punic War, one of the most brutal and pitiless acts of aggression in human history.

That the Carthaginians managed to keep from waging war for so long stands as a testament to their prudence and self-control. Almost immediately after the treaty ending the Second Punic War had been signed, Masinissa, now master of all Numidia, began harassing Carthage. Believing his alliance with Rome would protect him, for years he periodically raided Carthaginian towns and burned or took over his victims' fields and villages. In each instance, steadfastly adhering to its treaty obligations, Carthage appealed to Rome to intervene and arbitrate. Although never refusing to oblige, Rome almost always took its time and then, in a blatant display of favoritism, decided in Masinissa's favor. As Appian put it, when new hostile acts occurred, "the Romans again sent envoys to restore peace, telling them as before to help Masinissa secretly. They artfully confirmed Masinissa in the possession of what he had already taken, in this way."[66]

One of the worst incidents occurred in 154, when the Numidians forcefully occupied a disputed area west of Carthage. A small force of Carthaginians, unable to contain their outrage, fought back. Masinissa, now in his eighties but still vital and aggressive, retaliated by usurping the "Great Plains," a fertile farming area just seventy-five miles southwest of Carthage. According to Appian:

> Masinissa raised a dispute about the land known as the "great fields" and the country belonging to fifty [Carthaginian] towns, which is called Tysca. Again the Carthaginians had recourse [appealed] to the Romans. Again the latter promised to send envoys to arbitrate the matter, but they delayed until they reasoned that the Carthaginian interests were almost en-

tirely ruined. They then sent the envoys, and among others Cato.[67]

When he visited Carthage in 153, Marcus Porcius Cato, known to history as Cato the Elder, was, like Masinissa, in his eighties. Cato had fought as a soldier against Hannibal and had later become a general, a consul, and one of Rome's most popular and honored senators. Cato believed that the Carthaginians had gotten off too easily at the end of the war, and he had harbored feelings of vengeance against them for decades. He was also a very conservative and miserly individual who looked down on rich people who conspicuously displayed their wealth. Therefore, he was especially repelled by Carthage's leaders, who built their lives around acquiring money and material goods.

When Cato, as leader of the envoys, walked the streets of Carthage, what he

The conservative and influential Roman politician Cato the Elder, whose hatred and distrust of Carthage helped to bring about the Third Punic War.

saw filled him with rage. It was larger and more beautiful than Rome and boasted a magnificent harbor, long streets lined with six-story buildings, and a high fortified hill, the Byrsa, crowned with imposing public edifices. The streets were busy, the people happy, and everywhere was evidence of wealth and prosperity. For this city, which had nearly wiped out an entire Roman generation, now to enjoy such prosperity was too much for Cato. When he returned to Rome, he reported what he had seen and staunchly urged his fellow senators to take action against Carthage. It became his habit to end every speech, no matter what the topic, with the words *Delenda est Carthago!* ("Carthage must be destroyed!"). And many Roman leaders heeded Cato's message. In the view of Roman conservatives at the time, as the Picards explain:

> Carthage was the only great city in the western Mediterranean basin which was not under Roman control. Her population consisted of those groups of people [rich families or those with long military traditions, like the Barcas] which are always most prone to revolt. Furthermore, she could not bring herself to forgive Rome for all the suffering and humiliation which she had endured at her hands.[68]

Using Masinissa as a Ploy

Thus, perhaps as early as 152 B.C., Roman leaders made a secret and fateful decision. They would destroy their old rival and remove a grave potential threat for all time. All that was needed was pretext, a seemingly legitimate reason for attacking Carthage. A possible excuse presented itself almost immediately. When a new dispute erupted between Masinissa and Carthage in 152, for the first time ever the Romans settled it in favor of Carthage, forcing the Numidian to give up some of the land he had taken. This, of course, was a ploy designed to make the Carthaginians overconfident in their dealings with Masinissa. And the ploy worked. The following year, Masinissa attacked and laid siege to the Carthaginian town of Oroscopa, and a few months later Carthage's general, Hasdrubal (apparently unrelated to earlier leaders of the same name), decided to counterattack. In 150, on an arid plain somewhere in western Tunisia, Hasdrubal's forces, numbering about fifty-eight thousand, met Masinissa's, about fifty-five thousand strong. Incredibly, the aged Numidian himself appeared on the field in battle array. "Although he was eighty-eight years old," says Appian, "he was still a vigorous horseman and rode bareback, as is the Numidian custom."[69]

As the armies clashed in a day-long battle, a young Roman observer watched from Masinissa's camp on a nearby hill. He was Scipio Aemilianus, adopted grandson of Scipio Africanus, known to history as Scipio the Younger. The young man had recently made a name for himself fighting rebels in Spain, and his presence at this battle in Tunisia signaled that Rome was watching the event with great interest. This worried the Carthaginian Council, for it had knowingly violated the part of the treaty that forbade Carthage to make war without Roman permission. So, after the battle, which was largely indecisive, when Masinissa surrounded Hasdrubal's camp Carthage sent no rescue party. Donald Armstrong describes how

Roman soldiers cock a catapult during the siege of Carthage. Confronted by Rome's well-trained, well-supplied army and its expertise in conducting sieges, the city was doomed.

food gave out in Hasdrubal's camp, and water was scarce in those arid hills. Hasdrubal's men slaughtered their pack animals and their horses for meat; when that source vanished, they boiled their leather straps to eat. They began to die of hunger, thirst, and disease. . . . Despairing of escape or rescue by a force from Carthage, Hasdrubal finally agreed to surrender. . . . By the terms of the surrender, the staggering survivors were to leave the camp one by one . . . and to walk— as best they could—through a long corridor formed by their enemies. . . . [But] as the sick and starved survivors of Hasdrubal's army dragged themselves out of their camp, the Numidian cavalry massacred them.[70]

Out of Hasdrubal's force of fifty-eight thousand, only the general himself and a handful of men made it back to Carthage. There, the Council, hoping to appease Rome, blamed the whole affair on Hasdrubal and condemned him to death. Hasdrubal, however, managed to escape, along with some trusted officers.

In another attempt to avoid a confrontation with Rome, the Carthaginian Council twice sent ambassadors to Rome, asking what Carthage might do to make amends. And twice the Roman Senate sent them away with the vague answer, "You must satisfy the Roman people."[71] Fear began to mount in Carthage, for it became clear to city leaders that Rome was toying with them while methodically preparing for war. This fear grew into alarm when in February 149 B.C. the city of Utica defected to Rome and made its port facilities available to the Romans. Immediately, Carthage dispatched envoys to Rome with instructions to maintain the peace at any price, even unconditional surrender. But they were too late. When the Carthaginian delegation arrived in the Roman capital in March, the Senate had already declared war. The final chapter in the long death struggle between the two peoples had officially begun.

Rome's Humiliating Demands

Following the Senate's war declaration, in the spring of 149 B.C. a Roman force consisting of some eighty thousand infantry and four thousand cavalry landed near Utica. This formidable army was under the command of the consuls Manius Manilius and Marcius Censorinus. Publicly, their mission was to wrest control of Tunisia from Carthage; however, the Senate had given them secret orders not to return until Carthage had been destroyed. To instill fear in the enemy, the Romans began by waging a campaign of psychological warfare. They issued the Carthaginians a series of humiliating and cruel ultimatums, giving the impression that if these demands were met, the city might be spared. The first demand was for Carthage immediately to supply Manilius and Censorinus with three hundred children from the city's noblest families. These hostages, the Romans said, were to ensure that Carthage would do Rome's bidding in any upcoming negotiations. Though they feared the young hostages would never be returned, the Carthaginians felt they had no choice. Appian describes the terrible scene on the day of the children's departure:

> They sent their children [into Roman hands] amid the tears of the parents, the kindred, and especially the mothers, who clung to their little ones with frantic cries and seized hold of the ships and of the officers who were taking them away, even holding the anchors and tearing the ropes. . . . Some of them even swam out far into the sea beside the ships, shedding tears and gazing at their children. Others on the shore tore out their hair and pounded their breasts as though they were mourning the dead.[72]

The Romans never returned the children.

The Carthaginians then begged for an audience with the consuls. Granting the request, the Roman leaders lined up their whole force of eighty-four thousand men in full battle array. With trumpets blaring all around them, the humiliated Carthaginian envoys had to walk directly through these impressive ranks to the spot where the consuls waited. There, the envoys begged for peace, saying that there was no need for Rome to attack since Carthage had already surrendered. Censorinus then rose and said, "If you are sincerely desirous of peace, why do you need any arms? Come, surrender to us all your weapons and engines of war, both public and private."[73] The envoys replied that they needed their weapons to repel Hasdrubal, who had raised an army of twenty thousand men and was intent on punishing the city for having condemned him. Censorinus insisted that he and his colleague would take care of Hasdrubal and sent the envoys on their way. Soon afterward, Carthage surrendered armor and weapons for more than a hundred thousand soldiers, along with at least two thousand catapults.

West Overcomes East

In their conquest of the large Greek-ruled Macedonian and Seleucid kingdoms in the years between the Second and Third Punic Wars, the Romans gained a large degree of control over the eastern Mediterranean region. This eliminated any hope that Carthage might pick up substantial eastern allies in its final struggle with Rome. In his book Ancient Times: A History of the Early World, *historian James Henry Breasted offers this description of the Greeks' demise.*

"A year after the close of the Hannibalic [Second Punic] War, [King] Philip [of Macedonia] found himself without strong allies, face to face with a Roman army. By his unusual skill as a commander, he evaded the Roman force for some time; but in the end the massive Macedonian phalanx, bristling with long spears, was obliged to meet the onset of the Roman legions, with their deadly short swords and the puzzling divisions behind the lines shifting into unexpected positions which the phalanx was not flexible enough to meet. On the field of Cynoscephalae ('dogs' heads'), in 197 B.C., the Macedonian army was disastrously routed, and the ancient realm of Alexander the Great became a vassal state under Rome. . . . This war with Macedonia brought the Romans into contact with Antiochus the Great, the Seleucid king, who held a large part of the vast [former] empire of Persia in Asia; for Antiochus endeavored to profit by Philip's defeat and to seize some of Philip's former possessions which the Romans had declared free. . . . The conqueror of Hannibal [Scipio Africanus] . . . was with the Roman army to counsel his brother, another Scipio, consul for the year and therefore in command of the legions. There was no hope for the undisciplined [Seleucid] troops when confronted by a Roman army under such masters of the new [military] tactics as these two Scipios. At Magnesia [in Asia Minor] the West, led by Rome, overthrew the East, led by . . . Antiochus (190 B.C.), and the lands of Asia Minor eastward to the river Halys submitted to Roman control."

Once the city had been disarmed, the consuls summoned the Carthaginian envoys to hear still another demand that would have to be met for the sake of peace. The ambassadors stood with their heads bowed, waiting for some new humiliation. What they heard went far beyond their worst expectation. Manilius and Censorinus informed them that their people must leave Carthage immediately and begin building new homes at least ten miles inland from the sea. The Romans would then raze, or demolish, the city, including every house and public building. At this, the envoys, shedding their submissive manner, flew into a fury and cursed the Romans to their faces.

The Heroic Transformation

The reaction in Carthage to the final Roman ultimatum was also one of disbelief and outrage. At first, riots broke out everywhere as angry mobs attacked Council members and others who had advocated giving in to the earlier demands. When these disturbances died down, however, a new mood gripped the populace, one that had never been seen before in Carthage. In the past, the Carthaginians had cared mainly for wealth and had been content to let mercenaries do their fighting. Out of greed or fear, they had made many poor decisions that had brought their once mighty empire toppling down. Yet now, in this hour of supreme danger, they rose heroically to the challenge. "A wonderful change and determination came over them," says Appian, "to endure everything rather than abandon their city. Quickly all minds were filled with courage from this transformation."[74]

Thus transformed, the Council formally declared war on Rome, then freed all the city's slaves and declared them citizens. The rich families immediately gave up their wealth and, with their former servants, created a united force to defend the city. City leaders also sent envoys on bended knee to Hasdrubal, begging him to forgive the bad treatment he had received and come to his city's aid. In a show of character and courage worthy of Hannibal and other great past Carthaginian leaders, Hasdrubal agreed and began preparing to attack the Romans. Meanwhile, the people in the city made their own preparations, including the forging of new weapons. According to Appian's report:

> All the sacred places, the temples and every other wide and open space, were turned into workshops, where men and women worked together day and night, on a fixed schedule, without pause, taking their food by turns. Each day they made 100 shields, 300 swords, 1,000 missiles for catapults, 500 darts and spears, and as many catapults as they could. For strings to bend them the women cut off their hair for want of other fibers.[75]

The Romans were clearly unprepared for such a tremendous show of resistance. When they first attempted to lay siege to the city, the Carthaginians repulsed them, killing over five hundred legionnaires. The Carthaginians soon won other skirmishes and in a daring raid burned several Roman ships. Then, late in 149, Manilius decided to wipe out Hasdrubal's army, which had swelled to thirty thousand and was camped at Nepheris, some twenty miles southeast of Carthage. The overconfident consul led about thirty-five thousand men to an embarrassing defeat at Hasdrubal's hands. In the following year, low on men and supplies, the Romans stayed mainly near their camp while Hasdrubal roamed freely through the countryside, rallying the surrounding towns.

A City's Death Throes

But the Carthaginian cause, though steeped in gallantry, was doomed. Early in

Sound Advice Ignored

Hasdrubal's unexpected defeat of the Romans at Nepheris occurred because the Roman commander, the consul Manilius, was inexperienced and shortsighted. In this excerpt from The Reluctant Warriors, *a study of the Third Punic War, military historian Donald Armstrong explains how the young officer Scipio Aemilianus tried in vain to advise his superior.*

"Scipio urged Manilius, if he persisted in his offensive, to fortify a camp to which the Romans could retreat if they were overpowered. Scipio evidently had little confidence in this army: its morale, after six months in Africa and a series of unsuccessful assaults on Carthage, must have been low. . . . After the severe losses suffered in previous months, it is unlikely that Manilius led more than 35,000 infantry to the battlefield. Each legion, with approximately 3,000 men in three lines, formed a front of three hundred yards. Hasdrubal, looking down from his position, estimated the Roman front . . . at about a mile and a half long. . . . Hasdrubal's inferiority in numbers—he never had more than 30,000 men—found compensation in the river and in the steep hill up which the enemy had to advance. His camp and the ravine at the foot of the hill would ensure the success of his plan. . . . Manilius . . . gave the signal to attack. The trumpets sounded the charge. . . . [After much indecisive fighting, Hasdrubal withdrew into his camp, then unexpectedly exited, and attacked and overcame the Romans as they were marching away downhill.] Manilius by this time regretted his plan of battle: by now anyone could see the wisdom of Scipio's advice to build a camp for refuge in the event of a stalemate or defeat. Manilius had led his army into a trap from which only the most adept tactics could extricate [free] it without severe loss. But Manilius lacked that kind of adeptness."

147 B.C., the Romans temporarily suspended their law requiring a consul to be at least forty-three years old. This was done in order that their most prestigious general, Scipio the Younger, only thirty-seven, could be elected and then lead the war in Africa. Scipio arrived with reinforcements and took several weeks to regroup the Roman forces already entrenched. Fearing a siege, Hasdrubal left an officer named Diogenes in charge of his forces at Nepheris and returned to Carthage. Once Scipio had used some troops to surround the capital and begin the siege, he marched on Nepheris, easily defeated Diogenes, and thereby cut off Carthage's only source of outside aid.

The siege itself was long, desperate, bloody, and characterized by inhumane acts on both sides. At one point, according to Appian, Hasdrubal

> took the Roman prisoners whom he held, brought them upon the [city's] walls, in full sight of their comrades, and tore out their eyes, tongues, tendons, or private parts with iron hooks; of some he lacerated the soles of the feet, of others he cut off the fingers, and some he flayed [sliced open] alive, hurling them all, still living from the top of the walls.[76]

The Romans matched and then surpassed these atrocities. After months of relentless siege tactics, in March 146 Scipio's massive assault forces breached the city walls, and several days of desperate and cruel street fighting ensued. Every house was defended to the death by Carthaginian men, women, and children, and the carnage was horrendous. When Scipio's forces reached the Byrsa, reports Appian, they set fire to whole streets and

> then came scenes of new horror. The fire spread and carried everything down. . . . So the crashing grew louder, and many fell dead under the collapsing stones. Others were seen still living . . . some of them wounded, some more or less burned, and utter-

The Romans pillage and destroy Carthage in the terrifying conclusion of the Third Punic War. Those Carthaginians who survived the bloody carnage were sold into slavery.

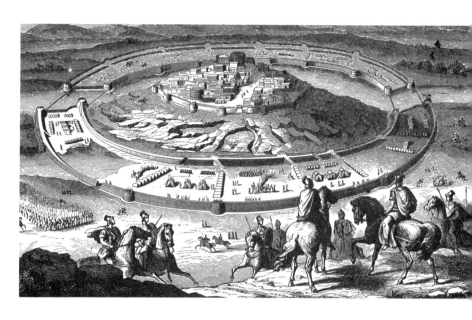

After capturing Carthage, the Romans burn the city. According to ancient sources, the fire raged for seventeen days and left little standing.

ing horrible cries. Still others . . . were torn asunder into all kinds of horrible shapes, crushed and mangled. . . . Some were thrown [by Roman soldiers] into [ditches] head foremost, while their legs, sticking out of the ground, wriggled a long time. Others fell with their feet downward and their heads above ground. Horses ran over them, crushing their faces and skulls. . . . Six days and nights were consumed in this kind of turmoil.[77]

Eventually, following the orders of the Roman Senate, Scipio set fire to the rest of the city and from a hillside watched the enormous spectacle of the city's death throes. At this fateful moment, the historian Polybius, who was Scipio's friend, stood beside the consul and recorded for posterity how

at the sight of the city utterly perishing amid the flames, Scipio . . . burst into tears and stood long reflecting on the inevitable change which awaits cities, nations and dynasties, one and all. . . .

Turning to a friend who stood near him, he grasped his hand and said: "It is a wonderful sight, but . . . I feel a terror and dread lest someone should one day do the same to my own native city."[78]

When, after seventeen days, the deadly inferno finally burned out, the Romans tore down what remained of the city's once impressive walls, docks, and buildings. They sold the surviving Carthaginians into slavery, sowed salt into the earth throughout the area to discourage future agriculture, and forbade anyone to build there ever again.

Thus did Carthage, one of the world's greatest cities, after seven centuries of life and unique cultural development, vanish forever. Thereafter, Carthage's former territory became the new Roman province of Africa, ruled directly from Rome. For peoples around the Mediterranean, the lesson of the Third Punic War was plain— Roman imperialism was unstoppable. In the same year that Carthage met its end,

Congratulations and Embraces

In this tract from his Roman History, *Appian tells how, after cruelly leveling Carthage, the Romans triumphed and enriched themselves at their victims' expense.*

"Carthage being destroyed, Scipio [the Younger] gave the soldiers a certain number of days for plunder, reserving [for the state] the gold, silver, and temple gifts. He also gave numerous prizes to all who had distinguished themselves for bravery. . . . He sent a swift ship, embellished with spoils, to Rome to announce the victory. He also sent word to Sicily that whatever temple gifts they could identify as taken from them by the Carthaginians in former wars they might come and take away. Thus he endeared himself to the people as one who united clemency with power. The rest of the spoils he sold, and . . . burned the [enemy's] arms, engines, and useless ships as an offering to Mars [the god of war] and Minerva [the goddess of Wisdom, often depicted in armor], according to the Roman custom. When the people of Rome saw the ship and heard of the victory early in the evening, they poured into the streets and spent the whole night congratulating and embracing each other like people just now delivered from some great fear, just now confirmed in their supremacy, just now assured of the permanence of their own city. . . . They recalled what they had suffered from the Carthaginians in Sicily and Spain, and in Italy itself for sixteen years, during which Hannibal destroyed 400 towns and killed 300,000 of their own men in battles alone. . . . Remembering these things, they were so excited over this victory that they could hardly believe it, and they asked each other over and over again whether it was really true that Carthage was destroyed."

the Romans also razed to the ground the Greek city of Corinth as a warning to would-be Greek rebels. Rome then imposed direct rule on the former Greek kingdoms. From Spain to the Middle East, nations once proudly independent like Carthage quaked in fear and then watched helplessly as the Roman eagle's great wings spread relentlessly outward and enveloped the known world.

The Legacies of Rome and Carthage

In a way, Scipio Aemilianus, final conqueror of Carthage, turned out to be a prophet. Watching the city burn, he had

Fear and despair grip Rome as the Vandals sack the city in A.D. 455.

felt a dread that his own city, Rome, might suffer similar destruction. Certainly, this did not happen in Scipio's lifetime, nor for many generations to come. After forever erasing Carthaginian culture, the Roman Republic went on to further conquests. In the first century B.C., however, power struggles and civil wars among powerful military leaders led to the fall of the republic, which was replaced by the Roman Empire. Ruled by a long succession of dictators, the empire continued to expand Roman borders until, by the second century A.D., Rome held sway over most of Europe, all of northern Africa, and much of the Middle East. This vast political unit, the largest in history up to that time, encompassed some 3.5 million square miles and perhaps a hundred million people.

Yet in time, this mighty empire declined and decayed. Beset by internal corruption and inefficiency, as well as by increasing external attacks on its borders, the Roman Empire fell apart in the fourth and fifth centuries. In the year 476, so-called barbarians from northern Europe drove the last Roman emperor from his throne and took control of Rome. The city that had once held a million souls and ruled the known world became a vast ghost town in which a few thousand poverty-stricken individuals squatted in crumbling buildings. Thus, Scipio's dire prediction came true at last and Rome, like Carthage, faded into obscurity.

Rome's cultural legacy remained, however. The Latin language evolved into or combined with other tongues to form the basis of many modern European languages. Roman concepts of law and statecraft deeply influenced the scattered, backward kingdoms that later grew into powerful European nations such as France, Germany, and Britain. And in its legacy Rome also passed on to later European cultures the magnificent arts, architecture, and literature of ancient Greece, which the Romans had so admired.

By comparison, Carthage left behind no cultural heritage for future generations. This was because its native culture perished almost completely in the climactic and savage Roman onslaught in the Third Punic War. Other peoples eventually resettled the site of Carthage, but they had nothing in common with the Phoenician-based culture that had occupied the region for so long. About a century after the city's demise, the powerful Roman general Julius Caesar lifted the restriction against building there. Under his rule and that of the first Roman emperor, Augustus, a Roman city called Colonia Julia Carthago grew upon the decaying ruins of the former metropolis. Roman Carthage became a prosperous trading center and popular tourist spot. It boasted fine public baths and an arena, seating eighty thousand, for gladiator fights and other sports. In the later years of the empire, as the new faith of Christianity spread rapidly, Carthage produced several bishops and also Christian writers such as the influential Tertullian.

In 439, as the Roman Empire was in its death throes, the Vandals, a warlike European people, crossed from Spain into Africa and overran Carthage. The city then swiftly declined into an uncultured pirate stronghold. It underwent a minor revival when Arab chieftains captured it in the 600s. But by the mid-700s, the site, now a mere jumble of stone ruins and wooden shacks, once more faded into obscurity.

As for the Numidian kingdom that had helped bring about Carthage's downfall, it too disappeared into northern Africa's dusty plains. Masinissa died shortly before Carthage's end, and his dream of a Numidia stretching from the Atlantic in the west to Egypt in the east died with him. A few decades later, a new Numidian war leader—Jugurtha—arose and made the mistake of challenging Rome. In what they called the Jugurthine War, the Romans crushed this upstart, and thereafter Numidia became, like so many other Roman victims, a mere memory.

Time and Circumstance

It was not until the nineteenth century that the cultures of northwestern Africa began to emerge from the dust and yield up their pitiful remains to the careful searches of scholars. The first modern excavations of the site of Carthage, at the time in the outskirts of the modern city of Tunis, took place in 1857. At first, the archaeologists had high hopes, for, as the Picards explain in their scholarly study *Daily Life in Carthage*, these investigators

> expected to find important remains of the chief Carthaginian buildings which are known to us through [ancient] texts, namely, the harbor works, the ramparts, the palaces, and the

temples. These hopes were soon shattered. With very few exceptions, all the ruins which were revealed then, as well as subsequently, in the Carthaginian peninsula, belonged to the Roman city built there one hundred years after the destruction of [Carthage].[79]

Since the days of the first excavations, diggers have repeatedly confirmed just how thoroughly Scipio did his job of razing the city to the ground. The only remains of native Carthaginian culture unearthed have been a few tombs hidden deep beneath the sands, containing little more than badly decomposed bones; some urns containing the ashes of children once consumed in the flames of human sacrifice, a practice that so horrified the Romans; a few isolated and badly ruined buildings and wall foundations; and a number of coins and crude shards of pottery. No Carthaginian literature, native histories, major sculptures and artistic works, religious temples, or other important artifacts have ever been found.

Did Carthage leave behind nothing of value for future generations? Perhaps without knowing it, Greek and Roman writers like Polybius, Appian, Livy, and Italicus preserved an important memory in their writings describing the Punic Wars. They recorded how, over centuries of hard work and struggle, an industrious and proud people climbed from humble beginnings to great heights of wealth and power. Then, just as spectacularly, they were annihilated by a power even greater than their own.

What lives on, therefore, is the chronicle of the Carthaginians' struggle. It is a

The decaying ruins of various ancient settlements built on the site of Phoenician Carthage dot the northern Tunisian coast.

stirring story that in a way transforms the landmarks of modern Tunis into markers commemorating the deeds of souls long forgotten. In Tunis today, writes Donald Armstrong, "The American ambassador lives just below the Byrsa. From the Byrsa's summit, the visitor sees the United States flag flying beside the ambassador's villa under the hill where the Carthaginians made their last stand in defense of their homes and their freedom."[80] Perhaps, then, the legacy of Carthage and the Punic Wars, like that of Rome's later fall, is a warning. It is a reminder to present and future nations that no human endeavors or monuments, no matter how splendid and mighty, are ever permanent. In the end, time and circumstance alter and erase them all.

Notes

Introduction: The Frightening Specter of World War

1. Polybius, *The Histories.* Translated by W. R. Paton. Cambridge, MA: Harvard University Press, 1966.
2. Dorothy Mills, *The Book of the Ancient Romans.* New York: G. P. Putnam's Sons, 1927.
3. Arleigh Burke, Introduction to Donald Armstrong, *The Reluctant Warriors.* New York: Thomas Y. Crowell, 1966.

Chapter 1: Ancient Rivalry: The Western Mediterranean on the Eve of War

4. Gavin de Beer, *Hannibal: Challenging Rome's Supremacy.* New York: Viking Press, 1969.
5. H. H. Scullard, *The Etruscan Cities and Rome.* Ithaca, NY: Cornell University Press, 1967.
6. Michael Grant, *History of Rome.* New York: Charles Scribner's Sons, 1978.
7. Grant, *History of Rome.*
8. Armstrong, *The Reluctant Warriors.*
9. Gilbert Picard and Colette Picard, *Daily Life in Carthage at the Time of Hannibal.* New York: Macmillan, 1961.
10. Quoted in Plutarch, *Life of Pyrrhus,* in *Lives of the Noble Grecians and Romans.* Translated by B. Perrin. Cambridge, MA: Harvard University Press, 1958.
11. James Henry Breasted, *Ancient Times: A History of the Early World.* Boston: Ginn, 1944.
12. Appian, *Roman History.* Translated by Horace White. Cambridge, MA: Harvard University Press, 1964.
13. Picards, *Daily Life.*
14. de Beer, *Hannibal.*

Chapter 2: Once More into the Breach: The Death Struggle Begins

15. Polybius, *The Histories.*
16. Polybius, *The Histories.*
17. Mills, *The Book of the Ancient Romans.*
18. Polybius, *The Histories.*
19. Gilbert Picard and Colette Picard, *The Life and Death of Carthage.* New York: Taplinger, 1968.
20. Polybius, *The Histories.*
21. Polybius, *The Histories.*
22. de Beer, *Hannibal.*
23. Polybius, *The Histories.*
24. Polybius, *The Histories.*

Chapter 3: Expansion by Naked Aggression: The Between-War Years

25. Breasted, *Ancient Times.*
26. Polybius, *The Histories.*
27. Polybius, *The Histories.*
28. Picards, *The Life and Death of Carthage.*
29. Cornelius Nepos, *The Book of the Great Generals of Foreign Nations.* Translated by John C. Rolfe. Cambridge, MA: Harvard University Press, 1960.
30. Livy, *History from the Founding of the City.* Translated by Frank Gardner Moore. Cambridge, MA: Harvard University Press, 1966.
31. Appian, *Roman History.*
32. Appian, *Roman History.*

Chapter 4: Daring, Fortitude, and Genius: Hannibal Invades Italy

33. de Beer, *Hannibal.*
34. Livy, *History.*
35. Silius Italicus, *Punica.* Translated by J. D. Duff. Cambridge, MA: Harvard University Press, 1961.

36. Polybius, *The Histories.*
37. Plutarch, *Life of Fabius,* in *Lives of the Noble Grecians and Romans.*
38. Grant, *History of Rome.*
39. Plutarch, *Life of Fabius.*
40. de Beer, *Hannibal*
41. Plutarch, *Life of Fabius.*
42. Livy, *History.*

Chapter 5: Rome's Unbroken Spirit: The Tide of Battle Slowly Turns

43. Quoted in Livy, *History.*
44. Mills, *The Book of the Ancient Romans.*
45. Lucius Florus, *Epitome of Roman History.* Translated by Edward S. Forster. Cambridge, MA: Harvard University Press, 1960.
46. Polybius, *The Histories.*
47. Quoted in Polybius, *The Histories.*
48. Polybius, *The Histories.*
49. Grant, *History of Rome.*
50. Livy, *History.*
51. Livy, *History.*
52. Quoted in Italicus, *Punica.*
53. Livy, *History.*

Chapter 6: Death at the Door: The Second War's Bloody Climax

54. Appian, *Roman History.*
55. Appian, *Roman History.*
56. Quoted in Livy, *History.*

57. Livy, *History.*
58. Polybius, *The Histories.*
59. Livy, *History.*
60. Appian, *Roman History.*
61. Polybius, *The Histories.*
62. Appian, *Roman History.*
63. Quoted in Livy, *History.*
64. Quoted in de Beer, *Hannibal.*
65. Grant, *History of Rome.*

Chapter 7: Carthage in Flames: The Last Days of a Great City

66. Appian, *Roman History.*
67. Appian, *Roman History.*
68. Picards, *The Life and Death of Carthage.*
69. Appian, *Roman History.*
70. Armstrong, *The Reluctant Warriors.*
71. Quoted in Appian, *Roman History.*
72. Appian, *Roman History.*
73. Quoted in Appian, *Roman History.*
74. Appian, *Roman History.*
75. Appian, *Roman History.*
76. Appian, *Roman History.*
77. Appian, *Roman History.*
78. Polybius, *The Histories.*

Epilogue: The Legacies of Rome and Carthage

79. Picards, *Daily Life.*
80. Armstrong, *The Reluctant Warriors.*

For Further Reading

Lionel Casson, *Daily Life in Ancient Rome.* New York: American Heritage Publishing, 1975. A fascinating presentation of how the Romans lived: their homes, streets, entertainments, eating habits, theaters, religion, slaves, marriage customs, government, tombstone epitaphs, and much more.

Harold Lamb, *Hannibal: One Man Against Rome.* New York: Bantam, 1963. A highly comprehensive and very readable telling of the Punic Wars, with a main emphasis on the second conflict and Hannibal's exploits. Somewhat advanced reading.

Anthony Marks and Graham Tingay, *The Romans.* London: Usborne, 1990. A beautifully illustrated summary of Roman history and all aspects of daily life, written for basic readers.

Don Nardo, *The Battle of Zama.* San Diego, CA: Lucent Books, 1996. Can be used as a companion volume to this one. The author provides much more detail on the battle in which Hannibal was finally defeated, as well as on Scipio Africanus and certain other aspects of the Punic struggle.

————, *The Roman Republic,* and *The Roman Empire.* San Diego, CA: Lucent Books, 1994. Comprehensive, easy-to-read overviews of Roman civilization, covering its entire span, from the city's founding in 753 B.C. to the empire's fall in A.D. 476.

Chester G. Starr, *The Ancient Romans.* New York: Oxford University Press, 1971. A general survey of Roman history with several interesting sidebars on such subjects as the Etruscans, Roman law, and the Roman army. Also contains quotations from many primary sources (ancient Greek and Roman writers).

Works Consulted

Appian, *Roman History*. Translated by Horace White. Cambridge, MA: Harvard University Press, 1964. The eleven surviving books of this second century A.D. Roman historian's twenty-four-volume telling of Roman history. These thoughtfully researched, clearly written materials remain essential reading for serious students of Roman times.

Donald Armstrong, *The Reluctant Warriors*. New York: Thomas Y. Crowell, 1966. A detailed, well-written summary of the Punic Wars by a noted military historian, with an introduction by Admiral Arleigh Burke (U.S. Navy, retired).

James Henry Breasted, *Ancient Times: A History of the Early World*. Boston: Ginn, 1944. Although somewhat dated, this extremely well researched, well-organized, and entertaining book remains one of the best general sources on ancient civilizations.

Gavin de Beer, *Hannibal: Challenging Rome's Supremacy*. New York: Viking Press, 1969. A detailed, somewhat scholarly, but fairly easy to read study of the Second Punic War. Contains several helpful maps, a feature missing from many similar histories.

Lucius Florus, *Epitome of Roman History*. Translated by Edward S. Forster. Cambridge, MA: Harvard University Press, 1960. Florus, of whom little is known, derived much of his material from Livy's history of Rome but undoubtedly used other sources now lost. Although the *Epitome* has an obvious pro-Roman bias, it is still one of the more important ancient sources on Rome.

Michael Grant, *History of Rome*. New York: Charles Scribner's Sons, 1978. Like Grant's many other studies of Greek and Roman times, this volume is very comprehensive, insightful, and well written. The section on the Punic Wars is certainly as fine an overview of that topic as can be found anywhere.

Herodotus, *Histories*. Translated by Aubrey de Selincourt. New York: Penguin Books, 1972. Although Herodotus's work focuses on the epic wars between the Persians and the Greeks, it contains many descriptions, some of them detailed, about the Phoenicians, the Italian Greeks, and the Carthaginians.

Homer, *Odyssey*. Translated by E. V. Rieu. New York: Penguin Books, 1961. The story itself, about the travels of the Greek hero Odysseus following the Trojan War, has nothing to do with Rome or Carthage. However, many scholars feel that the colorful and fictional land of the Cyclopes is a largely accurate historic view of the early undeveloped site of Carthage.

Silius Italicus, *Punica*. Translated by J. D. Duff. Cambridge, MA: Harvard University Press, 1961. This work by the first century A.D. Roman poet is the longest surviving Latin poem, containing about twelve thousand verses. The subject is the epic Second Punic War, including its heroes—Hannibal, Fabius Maximus, and Scipio Africanus. Difficult reading, recommended strictly for scholars.

Archer Jones, *The Art of War in the Western World*. New York: Oxford University Press, 1987. A scholarly study of the weapons and techniques of warfare in history. Contains excellent detailed descriptions of Roman soldiers and legions, as well as tactics and outcomes of several important battles, including Zama.

Livy, *History from the Founding of the City*. Translated by Frank Gardner Moore. Cambridge, MA: Harvard University Press, 1966. Of Livy's magnificent 142-volume study of Roman history, from the founding of Rome ("The City") to about 9 B.C., only 35 volumes survive. But these are among the most important ancient sources for the Punic Wars and many of Rome's other conflicts. Extremely worthwhile reading for those interested in Roman history.

Dorothy Mills, *The Book of the Ancient Romans*. New York: G. P. Putnam's Sons, 1927. This well-researched summary of ancient Roman culture, supported by many long primary source quotations, is old but not particularly dated.

Cornelius Nepos, *The Book of the Great Generals of Foreign Nations*. Translated by John C. Rolfe. Cambridge, MA: Harvard University Press, 1960. This important ancient source by the first century B.C. historian is similar thematically to, but smaller than, Plutarch's *Lives* and contains biographical sketches of Hamilcar Barca and Hannibal, among others.

Gilbert Picard and Colette Picard, *Daily Life in Carthage at the Time of Hannibal*. New York: Macmillan, 1961. A very detailed and scholarly study of Carthaginian customs, ideas, and cities.

———, *The Life and Death of Carthage*. New York: Taplinger, 1968. The companion book to the Picards' *Daily Life*, this equally scholarly study covers the political and social events of Carthage's history.

Plutarch, *Life of Pyrrhus* and *Life of Fabius Maximus*, in *Lives of the Noble Grecians and Romans*. Translated by B. Perrin. Cambridge, MA: Harvard University Press, 1958. Plutarch's biographies of important classical figures were based on many ancient sources that are now lost. Although the ancient author sometimes showed pro-Greek and pro-Roman biases, his works are thought to be reasonably accurate.

Polybius, *The Histories*. Translated by W. R. Paton. Cambridge, MA: Harvard University Press, 1966. A long and very detailed telling of Roman history during the period of the Punic Wars. Polybius, a friend of Scipio Aemilianus, who led the Romans against Carthage in the Third Punic War, was an eyewitness to the destruction of Carthage. This is ancient history come to life, and riveting reading. Highly recommended.

H. H. Scullard, *The Etruscan Cities and Rome*. Ithaca, NY: Cornell University Press, 1967. A scholarly study of the Etruscans and their important contributions to Rome.

———, *Scipio Africanus: Soldier and Politician*. Ithaca, NY: Cornell University Press, 1970. A very scholarly study of the famous Roman general who defeated Hannibal. Recommended for serious Roman history buffs only.

Index

Picture Credits

Cover photo: AKG, Berlin

AKG, London, 12, 18, 45, 51, 55, 78

Alinari/Art Resource, NY, 32

The Bettmann Archive, 11, 16, 27, 33, 85

Culver Pictures, Inc., 34, 54, 81, 93

Hulton Deutsch, 87

North Wind Picture Archives, 14, 17, 20, 22, 23, 30, 38, 47, 49, 65, 70, 77, 82, 95

Stock Montage, Inc., 39, 42, 62, 74, 92, 97

About the Author

Don Nardo is an award-winning author whose more than sixty books, many of them science- and health-related, include *Lasers, Gravity, The Universe, Ozone, Dinosaurs, Eating Disorders, Exercise, Medical Diagnosis,* and *Vitamins and Minerals.* A trained historian and history teacher, Nardo has produced several historical studies, among them *The War of 1812, The Mexican-American War, Braving the New World,* and *The U.S. Presidency,* as well as biographies of Thomas Jefferson, Franklin D. Roosevelt, and Joseph Smith. However, his specialty is the ancient world, about which he has written, in addition to this volume, *Ancient Greece, The Roman Republic, The Roman Empire, Traditional Japan, The Battle of Marathon, The Battle of Zama, Greek and Roman Theater, Cleopatra, The Age of Pericles,* and others. In addition, Nardo has written numerous screenplays and teleplays, including work for Warner Brothers and ABC-Television. He lives with his wife, Christine, on Cape Cod, Massachusetts.